Walking by Faith, Not by Sight:

The Mission of the Journey

Laina M. Brown

Laina M. Brown

Dedication

This book is dedicated to the loving memory of my aunt, Kerry Davis Byargeon, who inspired me to study English and use my words for good. Thank you for the last words you wrote to me before you left us suddenly. For those words are the most precious in the English language, "I love you."

Melinda Poitras, thank you for being such an inspirational person, not only to me but to so many others around this big world. A few years ago, you encouraged me to continue to write, and to always write what I know. Well, here I am with my biggest writing project to date. So, thank you for your voice, your words, and willingness to be used of God through your words. Your words (from God) are what have propelled me forward. Keep using those words, for you do not even realize your reach into the lives of others.

To Kayla: Thank you for being my sister by choice and best friend for life. There is no one else I would rather go adventuring with, laugh with, or cry with (though we both know you just distract me from my tears). You have always been my biggest fan whether you particularly like the idea or not. Although, let's not forget who always comes up with the ideas, dangerous or not, and the one of us that is the flame retardant. Thank you for loving me and putting up with me for 30 years of life.

To Taylor: The title of this book started in one of our many couch sessions, and now it has become a reality. Thank you for dreaming big with me even when I thought it was only a pipe dream and never going to take center stage. You are an inspiring and anointed young woman who has pushed me to be a better version of myself. Thank you for pushing me out of my comfort zone, though I might not have appreciated it at the time, I certainly do now.

To Melanie: Thank you for being the bright light that you are, and for showing me strength in the midst of trials. You are strong and courageous. Though life has thrown some curveballs your way, you have been strong and steady during the good and bad times. You have inspired me with your story. Thank you Mel and I love you always.

Finally, to my Mom and Dad: First, thank you for bringing me into this world and loving me unconditionally though I have not been the easiest child. Your encouragement and support have been a lifeline in my life during many tribulations. Thank you for your prayers and dedicating me back to God for Him to use me as He sees fit. Thank you for supporting the call of God on my life. I love you both with all my heart.

Contents

Foreword..7

Preface..9

Prologue...11

Chapter 1..17

Chapter 2..23

Chapter 3..27

Chapter 4..35

Chapter 5..41

Chapter 6..47

Chapter 7..53

Chapter 8..57

Chapter 9..67

Chapter 10...73

Chapter 11...85

Chapter 12...91

Chapter 13...95

Chapter 14...99

Chapter 15...103

Chapter 16...107

Chapter 17...111

Chapter 18...115

Chapter 19...121

Chapter 20...129

Author's Note...135

Acknowledgements..137

Foreword

This book has been a long journey in itself. It began as an idea in the fall of 2017. It became a tangible concept in 2018 though it was only half written. Then, it has long since sat dormant in a file until there was an urging in my spirit to finish it the beginning of 2021 through prayer and fasting. Now, this book has become a reality that does not seem real.

As a young girl, I knew I liked to write though I was not very fond of reading until senior year in high school. Early in my college years, I fancied becoming an author as I studied English literature. Never, until now, did I believe it would happen. It just testifies to the reality that anything is possible with God and when He begins a work in you, He is just to fulfill it completely.

As this book came to fruition, it slowly became another reminder of how beautifully God crafts and writes our story. He is the ultimate author and finisher. And though this book has a stopping point, the story is still being written by the greatest author. May the words from this book inspire and give Glory to our Lord for He is the one who has directed the journey from day one until now.

This book, *Walking by Faith, Not by Sight: The Mission of the Journey* was written with the intention to encourage others who may be on their own mission journey whether in life, missions, or ministry. Sometimes the mission of the call seems daunting, and the obstacles more than you know how to handle, but you must whisper to yourself, "I walk by faith, not by sight." So, in the deepest recesses of my heart, I pray that God can speak into your life through a small portion of my story. May God Bless you abundantly.

Happy Reading,

Laina

Preface

In the fall of 2014, I decided to apply for an Apostolic Youth Corps trip to Ireland for the summer of 2015. This decision was made after months of God tugging on my heart about Global Missions. I made this decision after I declared to never go out of my comfort zone again. However, if I were to get accepted, I would be going to Ireland, a place that I have always wanted to visit so the idea was a little less daunting. By completing my application for this trip, I was stepping out in faith. I prayed, "God, if it is your will then You will open the door, if it is not Your will then You will close it." God blew the door off the hinges when I was accepted for the AYC Ireland trip for the summer of 2015. This was to be my second missions trip, but my first foreign missions trip. This would be my first time to fly. I was so excited; however, I was very nervous at the same time. During the past few years of listening to God's leading, I learned to lean heavily upon my favorite Bible verse and what it truly means to not try to understand God's plans but to just follow wherever He may lead. In Proverbs 3:5-6 it says, *"Trust in the Lord with all thine heart; and lean not unto thine own understanding. In all thy ways acknowledge him, and he shall direct thy paths."* God has always been faithful to remind me of my favorite verses when my trust and faith began to wane in the light of obstacles.

Laina M. Brown

Prologue

Is there a beginning to a story? The answer is always "Yes" because as young children we were taught that a story must contain a beginning, a middle, and an ending. However, my story began before I was even conceived. It begins with a dream which later in the story will become even more significant.

My mother had a dream from God which came with instructions. Once, my cousin asked me, "Where did your name come from?" I answered honestly, "My mom had a dream and God spelled my name out in her dream." Do I know the exact details of the dream? Of course not. The dream was not my own; therefore, I can only relay what I have been told since I was a child. My mother's dream, which she had when she was pregnant with my older brother, consisted of her having a baby girl and naming her *'Laina'*. The spelling was vivid in her dream. She said she knew God sent her the dream because I wasn't even a thought in their minds at the time. She took it as God's promise to her and obeyed by giving me that name upon my birth.

My name is definitely unique and is rarely seen the exact way it is spelled, or without the typical 'A' in the front which creates the name Alaina. I love my name and the fact that it is unique. I wrote a blog titled "There is Meaning in a Name" where I mentioned that we each were given a name; therefore, also given a purpose. God clothed himself in flesh and was given the name Jesus; and He had the most important purpose of all which was to die for our sins so that we might be saved and join Him in Heaven one day. His name is the name above all names that we can call upon at anytime and He is there with us. My purpose of mentioning this blog is to remind you that we all have a purpose; and God began to reveal His purpose for my life through preachers speaking into my life at an early age.

After I received the Holy Spirit and was baptized at the age of eleven, it was just a couple of years after that I began to receive several words from preachers and evangelists that I would do a great work for the Kingdom. At that time, I was very young and did not write these specific words down but I have always remembered those words when they were spoken to me. Throughout my teenage years, I lived for God and stayed involved in the church, but I was not invested whole heartedly. I held back instead of going deeper in my walk with God. I struggled and spiritually I was not where I needed to be in my walk with God. To truly describe those teen years would be to relive years of self-esteem issues, bouts of depression, and fear and doubt in myself and abilities. However, with God I was an overcomer and without those trials and tribulations I would not be who I am today. My faith was built upon those trials, tests and tribulations.

One way God built my faith and elevated some of my self-esteem issues, was by answering a prayer which seems so trivial now but to me, it was everything at that time. Many young girls deal with self-esteem or self-image issues, so I pray that this story will help a young girl who doubts her worth. Your worth is established in Jesus. You are a daughter of the King of Kings. You, my dear, are precious. Never forget those words and never doubt who God created you to be.

This story begins in October 2007. I was sixteen about to turn seventeen in December. Well... you remember how I said I battled with self-esteem? During this particular time in my life, my insecurities were magnified, and I felt unloved, unwanted, and like a complete failure, not good enough. At that time in my life, it seemed as if everything hinged on me having a boyfriend. I had never had one which led me into thinking that I was unloved and unwanted. Therefore, when I could no longer bear it, God saw and heard me sitting in my living room, while my parents slept, crying out to God because I was broken and empty. All of the negative thoughts I had about myself were magnified as the negative thoughts others had said about my weight flitted through my mind. I was mentally depleted and drained by the time I finished crying and praying to God. However, after that night of weakness of begging God to answer my fervent prayer, I moved on with life and focused on enjoying the rest of my junior year in high school. Then, December came and with it my seventeenth birthday. Our town's Christmas parade was scheduled on my birthday, and our youth group had a float to enter in the parade. Some of my friends and I were dressed as angels for the parade that year. The interesting part of the entire night was that there was a new preacher's son who had began attending our church about a month prior, and he was riding on the back of our float with the other young people. Before that night, we had not really talked much, but that was the night everything changed. After the parade that night, I was at home talking to some friends on the phone when I mentioned that I thought I liked the preacher's son. It was the wrong thing to say to my meddlesome friends because they messaged him and gave him my number. The next thing I know, he calls me to talk and before we got off the phone, he asks me to our church's Christmas banquet the next night. Of course, I said 'yes', but that was not the only question asked that weekend. On Sunday night after our Christmas program, he walked me to my truck, and he asked me to be his girlfriend. The rest is history until three months later when reality came crashing down on what I thought was going to be a "fairytale ending". You see, God answered my prayer completely, but it was not meant to be a forever. Just as everything was going great in our relationship, we received the most devastating news a 17 year old in love could receive. His dad had received a position to pastor a church in Texas, and they would be moving to Texas the end of March. At the time, I did not understand how God could bring him into my life only to remove him a few months later. I was upset because I knew a long-distance relationship would not work for us. However, when he left, we tried to make a long-distance relationship work, but to be honest I was not able to handle it. He finally realized that it was not going to work and took the initiative to break off the relationship the end of May before it went any further. There were so many lessons learned from this relationship. God used this experience to show me that He heard my cries and saw my sorrow. On the other hand, through this relationship God showed me that a man could and will love me for who I am and not just consider my outward appearance. God showed me how a godly man should treat a woman through this relationship, and I will not settle for anything but the best because I am fearfully and wonderfully made by my creator and Savior.

David said "I will praise thee; for I am fearfully and wonderfully made: marvelous are thy works; and that my soul knoweth right well."

~Psalms 139:14~

As an adult with a closer relationship with God, I know that I have the ultimate loving relationship because my God loves me unconditionally and is always by my side. When I was younger, I thought I needed the love of a man to complete me, but God has shown me through patience that all I need is His love in my life to complete me and fill the void in my heart. I am whole through Jesus Christ. However, a few months after this relationship ended, God used a friend to give me the promise that He would send my partner in life one day. I have been holding on to that promise, 'walking by faith and not by sight'. I know that one day, in God's timing, that He would bless me with a husband to be in ministry with me as long as I kept the faith and stayed the course. My God has always been faithful to me; therefore, I am determined to listen to His words. His words, which says in II Corinthians 5:7, *"For we walk by faith, not by sight."*

Chapter One: Mission Beginning

As a Christian, now an AIMer, my story does not begin as a young child fascinated by missionaries who came to our church on deputation. In fact, I rarely remember having missionaries come to our church as a young child, probably because I was asleep under the pews like most children back in the day. You say I am only thirty that it was not back in the day; however, to me it was back in the day because I feel as if it was a long time ago. Anyway, back to what I was saying, I do not recall noticing missionaries who visited my church until my late teens and into my twenties. Those were the years God began drawing me out of my complacency and into the territory of uncomfortableness. Especially when He called me on that first mission trip to Lexington, Kentucky at the age of twenty. When I surrendered, I was the age of twenty one. I was finally going off by myself with no friends or family to be my crutch. It was such a scary time in my life.

I remember that first call to missions like it was yesterday. At the time, I believed God was just trying to give me a 'stroke' by pushing me out of my comfort zone. Thank goodness I was more afraid of what should happen if I did not listen to God than I was of having a 'stroke'. Now, I know it was the first step to the calling God was placing upon my life. He wanted me to take that step of faith and listen to His voice. This was the first of many more steps towards missions.

During this time, I was in the middle of my college career and I was struggling with what my future held in life and ministry. God had already used someone in the church to speak to me that I would be a leader not a follower. Well, that word from God for my life just made me even more frustrated because I was wondering a leader of what? I wanted, wait no... needed direction and clarity because I was very lost as to what I needed to do. With this state of mind, I found myself on my knees in our church's prayer room one Sunday night. My prayer was, "God, whatever you want me to do. I will do it. I want your will, your way. Tell me what you want me to do." God's answer was immediate. It was like a giant flashing neon sign, "Apply for the Louisiana District Missions trip to Lexington, Kentucky." My response was "Yes, Lord, I will go." That began my first step into missions and there was no turning back.

Applying for the trip took a step of faith, but the morning of the trip took even more faith and strength than I thought I had because fear tried to overtake me. However, with God I managed to overcome the fear, trust God, and get on the tour bus for my first adventure. Proverbs 29:25 says *"The fear of man bringeth a snare: but whoso putteth his trust in the Lord shall be safe."* By putting my trust in God, I knew I was safe because He was never going to leave me nor forsake me;

especially when I was walking in His will. In that moment, I had to let my fear go and put all my trust in God because this was the path He was leading me down. It was uncomfortable and painful to leave family and friends for seven days, but it was necessary to further my anointing and my walk with God.

Many times, we would rather stay right where we are because of the fear of the unknown. However, God did not create us to allow fear to keep us from doing what He called us to do. It says in His word, *"For God hath not given us the spirit of fear; but of power, and of love, and of a sound mind"* (II Timothy 1:7). Yes, fear of the unknown is an obstacle, but God has given us power to overcome and called us to walk by faith and not by sight. We may not be able to see what our future holds but we know the ONE who HOLDS our future. By having this knowledge, all fear and doubt should leave, and our faith should increase. God holds us in the palm of His hand and orders our footsteps. Therefore, if we have Faith in God then our future should never seem bleak or scary. This is a lesson that God has taught me many times because my flesh desires and longs for control; however, I am not the one in control of my life. God is the head of my life. And He orders my steps according to His mighty plan not the plans I try to make myself. Once we release the control over to Him, the worry, fear, and doubt fade away because our trust and faith is where it was always meant to be... In Christ Jesus.

The fear of the unknown on this mission trip tried to cripple me. If I would have allowed it to work, then who knows where I would be today. Most likely, I would not be in the perfect will of God for my life. This trip was the first of many to get me out of my comfort zone of Jonesville, Louisiana and to push me to be the Christian that I needed to be to fulfill my calling. In Lexington, I testified for the first time ever because I felt the spirit of God so strongly leading me to speak. Before I even made the move to go to the platform, I sat in my chair shaking with barely controlled sobs. Once I finally made it to the platform, I seemed to be rendered speechless from the uncontrollable shaking and crying but God helped me to finally tell my testimony to my peers and chaperones. Most of them were completely shocked that I even spoke because I was deemed the quiet one. For almost the entire trip that testimony was the most I had spoken at a given time because I usually only spoke when asked a question or it was absolutely necessary. Looking back, this quiet and timid girl has come a very long way in the past decade. God used that trip as a turning point in my life because now I am a girl who can speak to a room full of people without wanting to hide somewhere or without shaking so badly the words are mumbled. Most of the time I would rather fade into the background but remember when I said God called me to be a 'leader'? Well, leaders are in the forefront sometimes leading not in the background being timid and shy. God has spent years preparing me for my purpose and calling especially when I could not see what was in my future. Every step has been a part of the preparation stage for the calling and the purpose for my life that God planned since before I was born. Paul said in Ephesians 4:1, *"Therefore I, a prisoner for serving the Lord, beg you to lead a life worthy of your calling, for you have been called by God"* (NLT). Preparation is essential to fulfilling the calling because we must strive to be worthy of the calling God has given us. God has entrusted us, and we must lead a holy, surrendered life giving all of ourselves over to the ministry for God's Kingdom.

> *Reflection: Can you think of instances in your own life where God has pushed you out of your comfort zone for a specific reason or calling?*

God uses many different measures to prepare us for our calling and ministry. Every person's path is different; not one will be the same. Final destination may be the same but the path is always unique. Each person's trials and tests are like their own spiritual finger print. However, one thing remains the same for every person and that is we must ALL 'walk by faith, not by sight'. Remember, do not focus on the destination because only God can see the destination which is why walking by faith is so important; focus on the here and now which is the journey. Our life is a journey, one with purpose.

*"Who hath saved us, and called us with an holy
calling, not according to our works, but according
to his own purpose and grace, which was given us
in Christ Jesus before the world began"*

~2 Timothy 1:9~

Chapter Two: Limbo

"Wherefore seeing we also are compassed about with so great a cloud of witnesses, let us lay aside every weight, and the sin which doth so easily beset us, and let us run with patience the race that is set before us, Looking unto Jesus the author and finisher of our faith; who for the joy that was set before him endured the cross, despising the shame, and is set down at the right hand of the throne of God." ~Hebrews 12:1-2~

My limbo years consisted of the years when I came back from Kentucky and decided that I would never leave home again and step out of my comfort zone. That was until God worked on my heart when He drew me to Ireland. However, during these three years, I worked to finish college and I began my first job of teaching at my old high school. I continued to work in my church by being involved in almost everything I could be involved in. This was not good for my walk with God. Even though I was always doing something for the church and being a servant; my heart was not healthy because I was giving of myself but not taking time to refuel by being alone with God and continuing to build my relationship with God. Before I knew it, I had become burnt out.

As the verses say above, I was running my race, but I was piling weight upon myself that distracted me from looking to Jesus, the author and finisher of my faith. I was so busy with the work of the church, that I forgot why being involved in the work of the church was important. I became so engrossed with working in the church that it became a sin in my life because I allowed it to come between me and my relationship with God. Not only did I allow church activities to distract me, I allowed homework and social activities to be distractions as well. The sin in my life continued to grow because my foundation was no longer set upon our ROCK. As the years went by, the race that I was running slowly began to shift. It was no longer the race God set before me, but it was a race smoothly transitioning out of God's will. It was during these years that I began to no longer receive words from God. Oh, at the time, I did not even realize it because I was focused on my own agenda. However, sitting where I am sitting now, and knowing what I know now, how could I have ever believed everything in my spiritual life was good? I am thankful for a loving and merciful God who patiently waits upon us to wake up to the reality of our mistakes.

During this time, God reawakened my slumbering vessel through multiple means. However, there was a particular Sunday night after service where I sat in my car with friends and talked. I finally shared how I was feeling. I was tired of just going through the motions and being stagnant. When I voiced that, I began to be more aware and intentional to move forward and seek God. Never underestimate talking to those you trust. Perspective may be gained just by speaking and listening.

Since I became determined to listen, God directed my steps to another missions trip. This time it was an international trip. This time it would be thousands of miles away from my family and friends.

"A man's heart deviseth his way: but the Lord directeth his steps."

~Proverbs 16:9~

Laina M. Brown

Chapter Three: Ireland 2015

Reading through my journal from Ireland, I found that I had written this verse from I Chronicles 28:20, *"And David said to Solomon his son, Be strong and of good courage, and do it: fear not, nor be dismayed: for the Lord God, even my God, will be with thee; he will not fail thee, nor forsake thee, until thou hast finished all the work for the service of the house of the Lord"*, two days prior to leaving on this 10 day journey. Little did I know how much I would need to cling to this verse while in Ireland. Again, God amazed me because He used this trip as a growing process during a season when I was spiritually dead and empty on the inside. Remember, the limbo chapter? Well, this trip was the end of that limbo season in my life. I might not have realized it back then, but I had been running from my calling even though I was telling myself that I was only waiting on the Lord. But no, God was waiting on me to take action. In a sense, I was waiting on God, but I had allowed things to hinder my walk with God; therefore, He used this trip to help me knock down the walls I had erected in my life. God ordained the ministers and the words that were brought forth to speak into my life. Ireland was a wake-up call, and the beginning for a new and deeper walk with God. It is not a coincidence that two years later I would step back on Irish soil; this time as an AIMer living in Ireland.

Ireland was an indescribable experience. We experienced mighty moves of God, as well as battled some spiritual warfare while in the country. We spent most of our time in Belfast, a city in Northern Ireland.

During our time in Ireland, we were able to participate in services with four different congregations, as well as participate in the first ever Belfast Conference. Our trip was the largest AYC group, with over ninety people including the chaperones, so we were broken into two different groups to accommodate us on tour buses and at church services. God placed me with who He knew I needed to be around and the messages I needed to hear. Our first Sunday in Belfast, we went to Gilford for our morning service where one of our chaperones preached an anointed message titled "Perfected Praise" with his text taken from Matthew 21:14-15. That service was powerful because we had one receive the gift of the Holy Spirit and it was the missionary's son! The day was not over. We then travelled into Belfast for our afternoon service in a hotel conference room. God's presence was tangible in the service; however, I felt as if there was a wall keeping me from going deeper into God's presence. For our afternoon service, another chaperone preached a message titled "Stuck in a place called Haran." I still get chills when I remember that message he preached because it spoke into the depths of my soul. He took his text from Genesis 11:31-32 which states, *"And Torah took Abram his son, and Lot the son of Haran his son's son, and Sarai his daughter in law, his son Abram's wife; and they went forth with them from Ur of the Chaldeans, to go into the land of Canaan; and they came unto Haran, and dwelt there. And the days of Torah were two hundred and five years: and Torah died in Haran."* In this sermon, the minister discussed about not being complacent and staying in Haran, but pressing on and pushing toward the mark, toward Canaan. We cannot just come to Haran and stop, never moving toward the ultimate goal of reaching Canaan. Also, we cannot be lukewarm, or God will spew us out of His mouth as the Word states in Revelation 3:16. As christians, we cannot allow ourselves to die in Haran. If we allow our spirit to die in Haran then our flesh will reign and we will no longer be used by God. This sermon made me realize how flawed and stuck I had become. I was forced to reflect on my life and what I was truly doing to further the Kingdom of God. At this time, it reminded me that I was to be a leader. It also reminded me of a word spoken to me by my friend, Taylor, where she told me, "God has something special for you, Laina." God positioned everything perfectly to open my eyes to His plan and reassure me that I was worthy. I can hear Him speak and say, "Come out of the shadows my daughter and do the work I have set before you to accomplish." Oh, how joyous it is to serve the Lord with all your soul, mind, and strength.

From outreach to singing in the streets, we used our talents to be a blessing to the Ireland churches in the short time that we were there. However, one of the most impactful times of blessing to us was our time in prayer meetings in the hotel conference room and bus testimonial services. God's sweet and oh so powerful presence was a bolster to our souls and renewed us daily to witness in the streets of Ireland. I cannot say that I left a mark on Ireland, but Ireland surely left a mark on my heart.

During the time of witnessing and striving to be a light for Jesus in the midst of the darkness, I was struggling inwardly with my identity and specific calling. I knew God was calling me, but I had no direction or clarity from Him because I had erected a wall many years before to keep myself at arms length from God. Finally, I broke. I broke myself open before God, my heart was wide open. And my prayer was "Use me, oh Lord. Above all else use me. I give myself to you." When I prayed this prayer and sincerely meant it, God directed me to Proverbs 1:23-25 which says, *"Turn you at my reproof: behold, I will pour out my spirit unto you, I will make known my words unto you. Because I have called, and ye refused; I have stretched out my hand, and no man regarded; But ye have set at nought all my counsel, and would none of my reproof."* In my journal, my response to these verses was pleading. I said: "I felt as if God was sitting beside me reprimanding me because I have refused and questioned His leading before; and now I have not heard or felt His leading for a while. I must get it back, ask for forgiveness and begin to get my faith back because God can use me and will use me as long as I have the faith to believe and surrender myself completely to His will. I have to stop questioning God, stop fearing, and just act." However, this was not the end to what God had planned for me because He broke me once again during the Belfast Conference. Many things in my life had to endure a breaking, a breaking away.

"The Lord is nigh unto them that are of a broken heart; and safety such as be of a contrite spirit."

~Psalms 34:18~

The first night of the Belfast Conference was a powerful service, and the altars were filled. I prayed with my fellow AYCers, but then the tide changed when one of the chaperones instructed us to pray for someone who might be going through difficult times like us. I had two girls who prayed with me, and one of them gave me a small word from God, "He will fulfill the desires of your heart." And at that moment, another piece of my heart was cracked open because I knew in that moment that I was burying my deepest desire within myself to prevent myself from being hurt. It was a desire that God wanted me to give to Him, my desire for a marriage and family of my own. That moment I was broken again, crying, dependent entirely upon Jesus to make me whole again. However, the healing process was slow because God was in the process of changing and remolding me. After the service, I still could not fathom how I felt and just sat on the steps in the hotel staring off into space. A chaperone noticed and asked if I needed prayer, my reply was

I am fine though I definitely was not. He then spoke to my soul: "You have a sweet spirit, and God will use you and you are not unqualified." He knew that I was struggling, but all I wanted at that moment was to be alone with God. Once we arrived back at the hotel, I retrieved my Bible and sat alone in the hallway writing in my journal and talking to God. God gave me solace that night. I was prepared to seek after Him no matter the fears and doubts that plagued me because His word is my sword against them.

Night two of the Conference was phenomenal. We had thirty people receive the Holy Spirit. That night I prayed with a young boy to receive the Holy Spirit. I was completely out of my element as to what to say to encourage the young boy as he was seeking the spirit. However, God sent one of our chaperone's wives to be with us as he prayed, she prayed and encouraged both of us. After we prayed, I moved towards the wall, turned to face the wall, and wept before the Lord. I claimed victory and that the walls would be torn down in the Name of Jesus. I interceded on behalf of myself. I knew to move forward that I needed to gain sweet peace and lay everything on the altar before the Lord. Well, I laid it down but the next morning God spoke and said, "You did not give everything to me" in the form of the Sunday morning message. I previously asked God for a confirmation, or a message, and He provided one. The message was on harboring bitterness and resentment as well as making it through the storm to impact other's lives. Souls were depending upon me to make it through this storm and to pick up my cross. The last day in Ireland completely confirmed to me why God led me to come on this trip. For it is out of our comfort zones that God completely transforms our lives and provides our wake-up call to no longer be complacent where we are and in our walk with Him.

"Commit thy way unto the Lord; trust also in him; and he shall bring it to pass."

~Psalms 37:5~

When I returned home from Ireland, my church had begun revival with an evangelist. On my first Sunday night home, we had church for four hours. It was a powerful service, and many words went forth that night as well as chains were broken in the Name of Jesus. This service was a pivotal moment for many, but it was a special pivotal moment in my life. God gave me a direct word which began the first of many in the following years. I had finally broken through the storm I was in. The silence from God was over and it was time to go deeper than I had ever been before. The word came from my aunt who is an anointed woman of God whom I respect very much. She spoke, "God is leading you somewhere away but do not be afraid because He will be with you." Vividly, I remember just sobbing while she held me close to her when she delivered that powerful word from God to me. I knew right then that God's plans for my life were much bigger than I ever thought possible, and I was ready to surrender completely to His will. Running or being complacent were no longer options for my life, because I made the decision to walk in His perfect will. After service that same night, I went to my aunt to tell her thank you and give her a hug. She again pulled me close and said, "God was leading me somewhere and she did not know where, but she prayed it would not be very far away. And she told me to not go seeking it." This word has stayed with me over the years as I continued to follow God's leading and take the right next step for my journey. I only knew one thing at the time... big things were on the horizon, and I was going to follow God's leading no matter what may come. And a few months later, a last-minute decision had me applying for another Apostolic Youth Corps trip for the summer of 2016. At this time, I was not completely sure God wanted me to go on another mission trip, but I took a leap of faith and applied to go to the Spanish speaking country of Puerto Rico. With walking the path of missions, abounding faith is a necessity.

"But without faith it is impossible to please him: for he that cometh to God must believe that he is, and that he is a rewarder of them that diligently seek him."

~Hebrews 11:6~

Chapter Four: The In-Between

"Thou drewest near in the day that I called upon thee: thou saidst, Fear not."

~Lamentations 3:57~

When I returned home from Ireland, revival continued in our church for months. God completely brought us to another dimension in our church and many things changed throughout the end of the year. God changed me even more. This year was part of my wilderness years where I was steadily walking in my journey of life and God provided some manna to help me through.

Walking through the wilderness, I struggled but I held on to the promises and God's Holy Word. Fear and doubt plagued me, but God. I struggled with my singleness, but God. I had people sure of how things should be in my life especially who they believed my husband should be, but God is in control of my life, not people. God's ways are higher than our ways. In His word, He says *"For my thoughts are not your thoughts, neither are your ways my ways, saith the Lord"* (Isaiah 55:8). I had to remember this verse because there were many times that I would become discouraged. Discouraged about not understanding God's specific calling for my life, discouraged because I did not have God's perfect plan written down for myself to follow. And I allowed fear over being single the rest of my life bind me into not stepping forward into my calling. However, walking God's path for your life is not always easy, but it is oh so rewarding. I had to come to terms with the fact that I had to have faith that God would reveal His plan for my life in His timing and not my own timing.

There was a journal entry that I wrote during the year between Ireland and Puerto Rico. It was based upon a devotional that I had read, and it stated that there were three errors to avoid as we seek God's will: *1) Don't be fatalistic; 2) Don't be frustrated; 3) Don't be fearful.* And the main point it made was "The root problem is that you doubt God's love." That sentence still makes me want to weep because I was guilty of being fatalistic, frustrated, and fearful. However, did I doubt God's love for me if I was these things? I did not want to admit it, but maybe I did. I never would have thought that I would doubt God's love for me, but maybe I did if I had fear that overtook me when I was unaware. During this time, I wrote that I had many fears. One of those fears was the fear of the unknown in my future. At the time, I was so focused on what I was feeling that I did not remember God's Word which states, *"Take therefore no thought for the morrow: for the morrow shall take thought for the things of itself. Sufficient unto the day is the evil thereof"* (Matthew 6:34). It was hard for me to remember that God holds everything in His hands and that fear is not of God. This time was used to continue to mold me because I would need to make it through these trials and tests to withstand other tribulations that would be ahead. This journey of life was not easy, but God was with me on the mountain, and He was with me in the valley.

God has spoken to me many times to give me encouragement, and He has used my friends to do it. During a particular time when I was struggling, God spoke to me through my friend to reassure me that He was listening and that He heard my heart. It was during a church service that my friend, Taylor, sat down beside me, and leaned over to whisper, "I don't know what you have been praying to God for, but He is leading and guiding you. Something is about to happen in your life, you are going to be blessed." He is an on-time God. Just when we feel as if our prayers are only hitting the ceiling, He steps in to remind us that He sees and hears everything that takes place with His children. I hold on to the promise that He states in His Word, *"Therefore, my beloved brethren, be ye steadfast, unmovable, always abounding in the work of the Lord, for as much as ye know that your labor is not in vain in the Lord"* (1 Corinthians 15:58). If we continue to seek Him being immoveable and labor in His Kingdom, it will not be in vain because those that sow will reap a harvest in due time.

I was never alone even when I was struggling tremendously with the fact of my singleness. It seems that during a several month period I was battling thoughts of inadequacy and not being good enough because I had no one in my life to validate me by loving me. I knew that my value was not based upon having a man in my life, but it was something I had to battle and come out stronger than I was. I continued to learn that God was the only one who could make me whole and feel the void that I felt when I believed I was not good enough. Having to battle thoughts of fear, doubt, and self-worth became clear when I received a word from God through my friend, Taylor.

On Pentecost Sunday, we were in the prayer room before church praying, she leans over and says, 'I feel impressed to pray with you'. Taylor grabs my hand, and we begin praying together. I did not know where this was going to lead because I knew Taylor had a great anointing upon her. She has been used of God several times by giving me words directly from God. Then, she lets go of my hand and I thought that was it; however, thirty seconds later she leans over and whispers words that said, "God has not left your side. He is getting ready to give you great anointing that you have never felt before. It will be in God's timing and He is preparing you. You have to thank Him for what He is going to do and for the anointing. Thank Him. Thank Him." In that moment, I began thanking Him. I knew that great things were going to happen in my life, and that through everything He was preparing me for greater things. That word was the exact word I needed after months of discouragement and fear. God always knows what we need, exactly when it is needed in our lives. Trusting and following God always brings new revelations and joy unspeakable.

"Don't worry about anything; instead pray about everything. Tell God what you need, and thank Him for all He has done. Then you will experience God's peace, which exceeds anything we can understand. His peace will guard your hearts and minds as you live in Christ Jesus."

~Philippians 4:6-7 (NLT)~

Laina M. Brown

Chapter Five: Puerto Rico 2016

Puerto Rico was never my first choice for an AYC destination in 2016. I originally wanted to go to Spain because I always loved Europe and had a fascination. But, Spain was too expensive, and so Puerto Rico was the next best choice. I had a desire to experience a different culture with a different language. I was very hesitant to apply for another trip, but I did anyway and my prayer was "God, if this is your will then you will open the door." When February 2016 came, God opened the door, and I was accepted to go to Puerto Rico in June of 2016.

Puerto Rico was quite a different experience than Ireland. For one, we all could ride on the same bus because there was only fifty of us. I learned quickly that I was out of my element by only knowing a few phrases of Spanish, but I did the best that I could. It was a great learning experience.

We spent ten days on the Island of Puerto Rico ministering in and out of their churches. We had two services on the streets where the choir, composed of all young AYCers, sang in English and Spanish. We passed out invites to church services in different cities in Puerto Rico. During this time, God pushed me further out of my comfort zone especially when I testified the first Sunday we were on the Island. A funny story about me testifying is when the chaperones asked me to testify, my head said 'No' but before I got out no, my mouth and said, "YES". Needless to say, I was stunned but I quickly got over my shock because the service began. God gave me the words that He wanted me to speak to the congregation. During the worship service, God reminded me of a verse of scripture that my pastor says which is *"Enter into his gates with thanksgiving, and into his courts with praise: be thankful unto him, and bless his name"* (Psalms 100:4). I used that scripture when I testified, and it was perfect for the service. I may not have wanted to speak, but God wanted to use me as His vessel to speak that day. That was the first step out of my comfort zone that week and it was not the last.

While I was in Puerto Rico, God began opening my eyes and speaking as I was reading His Word. One morning, I was reading and came across Psalms 51:17 which says, *"The sacrifices of God are a broken spirit: a broken and a contrite heart, O God, thou wilt not despise."* The words *'a broken and a contrite heart'* stood out for me so I dug a little deeper. In the New Living Translation, it states *"The sacrifice you desire is a broken spirit. You will not reject a broken and repentant heart, O God."* Therefore, when we come to God with the broken pieces of our heart and a repentant attitude, He will take the brokenness that came from the sin of this world and repair the damage. He will repair our hearts and put the pieces back together again, but with a newness we have never experienced before. This verse reminds me of a song called "When I lay my

Isaac Down". The lyrics of the song say, *"And when I lay my Isaac down/With a broken heart but my Fathers proud/And n this altar here he lay/Just to find it wasn't him/God wanted me."* We may have hindrances in our lives that are holding us back from fully surrendering to God. But God is saying 'give it to me', 'give me the brokenness for I can heal you and make you whole.' We need to give it over to God, sacrifice or lay it upon an altar so we can completely surrender to God with no hindrances. As I reflect upon my experiences and walking with God, He tried repeatedly to speak to me about surrendering myself to Him, and let Him heal and deliver me. What God really wanted was for me to lay myself upon the altar so He could remold me into who I needed to be. Puerto Rico was part of the experience that I needed so God could prepare me and speak into my life.

During our second service of the trip, God did speak through others directly to my heart. Our first Sunday night service, one of our chaperones preached a fantastic message that touched the hearts of God's people, but it was what happened at the end of the altar service that spoke directly to me and my fellow AYCers. The presence of God was thick in the atmosphere. Many AYCers were seeking God whole-heartedly, desperate for a touch, a word, a deeper connection. The minister had discernment and God led him to have the AYCers pray for one another because there were some us of who came uncertain of their identity and calling. At this time, a lady came and prayed with and for me, she laid her hands upon my shoulders—I wept—for the words she prayed spoke into my spirit. No doubt her words were directly from the throne room. Then, all of us were still praying earnestly, another word was spoken by the minister—"God is working in your life; You have to trust Him. He has never left nor forsaken you. Your will should be His will. Leave here glad for God controls the outcome." This word gave me hope that God is working it all out for my good, and He is working on me during the wilderness I was experiencing at the time.

Fear and doubt continued to plague me throughout this trip to hinder what God wanted to do in my life and reveal unto me. My mind would try to focus on what the future would hold, and therefore it created a fear of the unknown. My mind would begin to reason all the reasons why I could not be used, and why I was not qualified which created self-doubt. Fear and doubt have always tried to keep their handhold on my mind, but I refused to allow them access, so God and I went to battle. I prayed, "God, I give the reins over to you. Take them and help me fight this battle again. God, use me and prepare me for your will. I know that if I can make it through the rest of this desert, wilderness, then I can make it through anything. For this has been a long battle and I am ready to come out victorious. I am ready for the next chapter of my life to begin. It has always been my prayer for you to prepare me, use me, lead and guide me down the path you want me to take. God, I am in need of you.

Heal me, restore me. Every day I will rebuke the fear, doubt, and unbelief in myself. I know once I come through the fire, you will lead me and direct my next step down the path you want me to take." Our God fights on our behalf and is a faithful and timely God. His word is not slack concerning His promises.

> *"The Lord is not slack concerning his promise, as some men count slackness; but is longsuffering to us-ward, not willing that any should perish, but that all should come to repentance."*
>
> *~2 Peter 3:9~*

As our time ended in Puerto Rico, we witnessed several filled with the Holy Spirit, experienced mighty moves of God in street services, and many of us left with unforgettable experiences and memories of our time there. One unforgettable memory was the amazing all night testimony service that we had our last night in Puerto Rico. Over that one week, we became a family, bonds were formed even though we may not speak still today. We are brothers and sisters in Christ; therefore, we will always be family.

After spending the week in Puerto Rico, I walked away with more direction and clarity as well as a closer sense of where I was called. I gained a closer walk with God, but He also opened my eyes that I was not called to a Spanish speaking country. Sometimes the way God leads us is by showing us what is not part of our call by allowing us to experience it for ourselves which in return allows us to grow even more. This trip stretched my boundaries and built my faith for future endeavors for God.

"Jesus answered and said unto them, Verily I say unto you, If ye have faith, and doubt not, ye shall not only do this which is done to the fig tree, but also if ye shall say unto this mountain, Be thou removed, and be thou cast into the sea; it shall be done."

~Matthew 21:21~

Chapter Six: Unite 2016 Youth Rally

The month before our Unite Youth Rally in September, I wrote a blog post titled "Where Do I Go From Here?". It conveyed the emotions and indecision I was dealing with in my life at that time, and it showed how only a month later, God spoke into my life and gave me the direction I was seeking.

Blog post: Where Do I Go From Here?

If you are like me, many of you have asked yourself the question, "Where do I go from here?" This question has been circling around in my head for a few days if not for a few weeks. Most would say that the only place to go from here is up, but I have to disagree with them. What about the other directions: right, left, down? Now, I do not mean down as in the literal since of the word but rhetorically speaking. Any direction could alter our lives significantly for the good or for the bad. Our decisions have many repercussions and can affect not only us but the people around us that we care about.

In Psalms 23, David says that God "leadeth beside the still waters and leadeth in the paths of righteousness for His name's sake." Also, in Proverbs 3, it says "He shall direct thy paths". To me these are all promises from God that He is in control; however, we are all human, correct? And our human nature is to question everything... Why this or why that? We do this because we must have the answers before we take that leap of faith. God, you know that I am guilty of this. I want to know all the answers right now, I want to have them written down in front of me. This is what we want but this is not how God operates because He expects us to trust Him with our lives and the path of our lives.

> "Trust in the Lord with all thine heart; and lean
> not unto thine own understanding."
> ~Proverbs 3:5~

Even though this is one of my favorite scriptures, it is very hard for me to practice it because I want to know every detail and want to understand in my own fleshly way.

God has been revealing certain aspects of my life to me slowly over the past few years and let me tell you, it has not been easy for me to accept how He has chosen to reveal these potentially life altering aspects. However, there is one thing we have to understand that it is all in God's timing and not ours. If it was our timing, it would happen now and happen fast. Sometimes God has to get us to a point where we are prepared for certain revelations in our lives. I am going to use some examples from my life. A few years ago, God had someone speak into my life that I was supposed to be a leader not a follower and at that time it was a foreign concept to me because I was still very shy and used to not being noticed. Now, after three mission trips and becoming *a teacher, I can see how I am supposed to be a leader. You see, God chooses specific timing to reveal His will for our lives or He chooses to not reveal His will or calling because He deems us not ready or not yet prepared.*

Ever since God revealed to me that I was supposed to be a leader, I questioned a leader of what. What type of leader did He want me to be? I did not get my answer until a few years later, just recently actually when God revealed to me what part of my calling was. And that calling is to be a minister's wife. Ever since God revealed this, I have had fear and doubt come into my life, and I was questioning whether God was the one who gave me this calling or if it was just wishful thinking. But God spoke to me again this past Sunday night and told me to quit doubting and questioning; which is what I plan to do. I will believe and have faith that God is working it out. However, this leads me to my beginning question "where do I go from here?" I have received my calling but what am I supposed to do with this knowledge because I do not have a prospect for a husband as of right now. And I just received a blessing in my career. God is orchestrating things in my life but right now they do not add up in my mind; especially if I factor in the fact that last year my aunt gave me a word from God that He was leading me somewhere and she did not know where, but she prayed it was not far.

All of our situations are different, and we do not know what the other is going through, but we have all asked the question "Where do I go from here?" You may be questioning other things that are happening in your life and do not understand how God could abandon you or you believe God does not care what you are going through. Let me tell you that God knows exactly what you are going through and He is there leading you even if you do not feel Him. Sometimes we have to go through the muck and mire for Him to reveal His plan for our lives. God also sometimes leads us through the fire to prepare us and make us stronger for the other things that are up ahead on our journey. We can question but we will never understand God's ways because they are not our ways and we will never understand God's timing in our lives. We just have to trust that He is never late but always on time. He is an on-time God. And if you continue to pray and see the questions that you have such as "Where do I go from here?" will be answered when He is ready for you to have the answer. Keep praying and keep trusting for our God will never let us down.

During this time of contemplation, I realized that I did not need to know every step because God wanted me to walk in faith by not knowing what the future held. I chose to take it day by day and trust His timing. Then, God began speaking and leading me on my journey. By surrendering my life, doors and words came forth to lead and guide me down the right path. Though I completely felt God was speaking into my spirit about my future at this time during my life, God's journey for my life has not yet led me to become a wife, but I still trust God in all things whether I fulfill my call as a single woman or as a wife.

In 2015, our church began having a Unite Youth Rally to be held every year in September. The concept behind the rally is to unite all the churches around our area for a common purpose and to allow young ministers a platform to preach. Every year we have four ministers or evangelists who have just started their preaching ministry to preach for the youth rally.

Our 2016 Unite Youth Rally was only our second rally, and it was amazing. Our closing preacher brought the house down with a great word from God. During his message, he gave a testimony about his brother. The service was amazing, the singing and preaching were phenomenal; however, I was struggling with my faith and my purpose. I was at an impasse again as I was desiring more confirmations about my calling and the direction of my life. There was a wall that I could not break through to see what God wanted me to see. As I was praying for others in the altar, the tide changed and people and the ministers began to pray for me. I was speaking in that heavenly language unto God asking Him "What was my calling, what did He want me to do?" One of the preachers came, laid their hand on my head, and prayed, "God, give her your word, show her what she seeks, reveal it unto her right now God." In just a few seconds, the wall dropped and the word 'missions' came across my mind. Right then, I knew that God had given me my calling, or He had confirmed within my soul that missions was my path.

You see up until this night, I was battling whether to register for Global Connextions and whether my next step should be to apply for the Next Steps program in the summer of 2017. By God giving me that one word, I registered myself and my friend, Taylor, for the Global Connextions seminar in St. Louis, Missouri in October 2016. I had already taken a step towards the process of Next Steps by talking to my pastor and he was not keen on the idea at the time, but suggested that we pray about it. Then, the Global Connextions weekend began, and it renewed a desire that had been birthed in my heart.

"Therefore I say unto you, What things so ever ye desire, when ye pray, believe that ye receive them, and ye shall have them."

~Mark 11:24~

Chapter Seven: Global Connextions

2016

Global Connextions weekend was filled with first-time experiences which impacted not only my life, but that of hundreds who attended any of the services or sessions that weekend. It was the first ever missions event dedicated to help this generation discover, prepare, and go. At this event was where I received a boldness to take a leap of faith to go deeper into the field where I was being called.

When my friend Taylor and I arrived in St. Louis from driving half the night, I penned these words in my journal before the conference even began. I said, "Many times I have faced disappointments and uncertainties within my life. All of these have been lessons learned along life's journey and for the path God is leading me down." Much to my surprise, I did not realize that God would use this event to confirm another journey to be taken on God's path for my life. God truly had me walking by Faith when I wrote my pastor a letter explaining my desire and the leading to apply for Next Steps: Scotland when I returned home from St. Louis.

Anyway, let me take a step backwards to the events of the weekend in St. Louis. When Taylor and I stepped into the church that night, we were introduced to the most enchanting individual who shined with God's love. At that moment, I did not realize how important that connection would become in my life though brief the introduction was with her. The first service was the Friday night where the Urshan choir ushered the presence of God into the service. The Lord moved in a mighty way, and the Lord began dealing with my heart. The next day, we had an experience of going through security and customs to be able to participate in the walk-through of the different regions to experience their culture. My friend and I enjoyed getting to learn through that interactive experience. I was given the opportunity to learn about Next Steps, and she was given the opportunity to learn about Medical Missions. At this point in the day, the desire to apply for Next Steps was growing in my heart then we had lunch with a missionary. Her stories of El Salvador and the work they accomplished had me sitting in awe of the journey God led them on. After lunch, we had the Prayer for the Nations session which was powerful in and of itself. However, the next sermon and speaker was by far my favorite of the entire weekend.

A great man of God preached the closing message of the conference that Saturday afternoon titled "Your Journey to Mount Moriah." That message impacted my life so much that I still tear up thinking about its resonating message. He was so raw to describe his own journey to Mount Moriah, and it grabbed my full attention because I knew God was using it to speak to my soul. God also used this couple to speak into my life when they were one of our chaperone couples in Ireland in 2015.

During the message, he discussed his first journey to Mount Moriah when he was elected as Secretary of the General Youth Division, and he was asked to give up his dream to follow God. And then he discussed how just three weeks before the conference, he had to return to Mount Moriah because he had aged out of the General Youth Division. This message was when I realized, God had a different dream than I had for myself, that His plans for my life were bigger than I had for myself. This time God was dealing with my heart to let go of the things that could hold me back from His calling on my life. I had to lay idols in my life on the altar: my job, my car, and my family. I had to make a decision to follow God's calling and not stay in my comfort zone. I had to lay my fear at the altar, my doubt at the altar, my comfort zone at the altar. When I laid it all down, I took that step of faith to follow the direction God was leading me in. At this moment, I decided to walk by faith and not by sight because God had ordained my steps to be in the right place to hear His words spoken through the minister. God will never abandon nor forsake us, because He has a purpose for each of our lives. He will lead us down the path, and the path will have trials, but through those trials is how we gain the anointing we will need in the future to survive yet another trial.

Global Connextions was another turning point in my walk with God when God pushed me to take the Next Step in my mission journey. God was calling me to missions and leading me step by step down the path to missions.

> "The Lord is my shepherd; I shall not want. He maketh me to lie down in green pastures: he leadeth me beside the still waters. He restoreth my soul: he leadeth me in the paths of righteousness for his name's sake. Yea, though I walk through the valley of the shadow of death, I will fear no evil: for thou art with me; thy rod and thy staff they comfort me. Thou preparest a table before me in the presence of mine enemies: thou anointest my head with oil; my cup runneth over. Surely goodness and mercy shall follow me all the days of my life: and I will dwell in the house of the Lord for ever."
>
> ~Psalms 23: 1-6~

Chapter Eight: Next Steps Application & Process

God was leading me step by step. And my next step was to go on Next Steps, but I needed to get my pastor's approval to apply for Next Steps. I decided that since I could not talk to my pastor and convey where I believed God was leading me, then I would write him a letter. I have always been able to write what was on my heart better than speak my heart, so it was the perfect solution. And it allowed him the time he needed to pray and talk to God about whether it was His will for me to apply.

On November 10, 2016 when I was at work, I received a text from my pastor that said, "I will get this form filled out and mailed in within the next few days ☹. We will miss you being gone that long, but God's business comes before our personal feelings." This text was the beginning of a new chapter for me because God was opening a door that I thought might remain shut. However, I took that as my sign, and I mailed my application in to Global Missions for Next Steps: Scotland 2017. The next step of the process was to wait for approval. It was a long month and a half before approval came, but I was not idle during that time.

After Christmas, I went with two of my friends to attend Mid-winter summit in Mississippi. I was only going to be there for one night service because the next day I was leaving with my family for a New Year's trip to Tennessee. When we sat down in the church service, I received an email from headquarters that they had received everything for my Next Steps application and that it was being reviewed. I was overjoyed because I had been waiting. I needed just a little good news which sparked a later conversation with a girl I had just met. God never ceases to amaze me how He orchestrates every move we make to have an impact and to connect us with people that we need or vice versa. Taylor had been invited to this summit through friends she met on her Hope Corps trip to Honduras. Therefore, I went with her and our other friend to Mississippi for the event.

That church service was amazing, and God's glory filled that place. During altar service, I had someone come and pray for me which I needed to give me hope and strength. After service was over, I was introduced to Taylor's friends and we walked over to their fellowship hall to eat. Another connection was made because I was introduced to Kimberly who happened to be a cousin to one of Taylor's new friends. We all walked back over to the church to get coffee from the coffee shop. Kimberly and I began talking about different things, and she mentioned missions and Next Steps. I asked, "Have you applied to Next Steps?". She said, "No, but I have always wanted to go, and I have been praying about it." Then, I told her how I had already applied and just received my email that they were reviewing my application. Then, I shared with her a little bit about my background in missions. And I urged her to continue praying about it and apply if she could. God brought our paths together that night so we could meet, and a friendship could be formed for the coming months. I knew that after I had that conversation with Kimberly that this was the reason why I had to come that night. A few nights earlier I had decided not to go because it was going to be a hardship to leave the next morning to drive back home before we left for Tennessee; however, I did not have peace about that decision, so I went. I will say that He leads us in the paths of righteousness for His name's sake. That night, that connection was meant to be made.

The new year had begun and there were new adventures that had not been discovered yet. The first new adventure for 2017 was attending all of the BOTT night services for the first time. I had bought my own pass so I could specifically attend the night services. Before the first night's service, I wrote a journal entry which used this verse, *"While we look not at the things which are seen, but at the things which are seen are temporal; but the things which are not seen are eternal"* (II Corinthians 4:18). In that journal entry, I simply wrote 'materials fade but God's love is never fading.' I also wrote some transparent thoughts which I am going to share below because when I reveal what took place next all the glory will be to God.

59

Laina M. Brown

Journal Entry

I took a step in faith and now I am in that waiting room again, the waiting period. I am trying to be patient, but I am ready to find out whether Next Steps is God's will. I know that this summer I will be going somewhere without a doubt, but in what capacity I do not know. Once again, I am battling with my flesh on the subject of my singleness. This is the time of the year that I struggle because of holidays and family functions where it is brought to my attention by family. It also does not help that I am a year older. However, I refuse to dwell on that fact. I will wait upon the Lord. Tomorrow, I will attend BOTT services for the next two days. Next year, if I am able, I will take off a day or two to attend day services and stay in Alexandria if I need to.

Take notice that in this journal entry, I mentioned about waiting for an answer about my Next Steps application and becoming impatient. Not long after I finished writing this journal entry, I received a Facebook message from the Director of Education/AIM. He messaged me to tell me that I had been accepted into the Next Steps program! My God is an on-time God! All the glory goes to Jesus! He heard the prayers of His child and answered quickly.

I attended the first night of BOTT right after I found out about my acceptance into the program. That night I was able to sit beside my pastor and his wife. I told them the great news that I had been accepted to go to Scotland/UK for two months of the summer. My next step into missions was before me, and I was walking through that door full steam ahead. The BOTT service was amazing with great preaching, and I was looking forward to the other two services. However, the next morning I awoke to begin another day of work, but I was not feeling well. I can still remember the nauseous feeling I had in the pit of my stomach and the dizziness I had. I told my mom that I did not feel right then went to the bathroom. I knelt on the floor, my vision went blurry, and then I woke up laying on the floor not knowing how long I had been there. My mom knocked on the door, came in and said you are as white as a sheet. Needless to say, I did not go to work that day; my mom helped me back to bed. I even tried to go to work the following day, but I could not make it through the first hour. A co-worker had to bring me home because I was so dizzy that I could not see straight. We never figured out what was wrong with me, but looking back on those few days I believe that it was a spiritual attack on my health because of my acceptance to the Next Steps program. The devil had a right to be scared. God's chosen are fierce warriors who are ready to fight and bring down the devil's strongholds. A new spiritual battle had begun from that moment until God's new step in my life was fulfilled and even beyond that step.

Over the next couple months, I prepared for Next Steps and helped Kimberly prepare as well since she had applied and was accepted too. My faith was under attack; fear and doubt were coming against my mind again. On a Wednesday night in March, an evangelist came and ministered to our church. He preached a sermon titled "The Power of Possibilities." During altar call, the evangelist came to me and said, "God told him to come pray for me, but he did not do it because he was hesitant." However, God called a second time, so he came to pray with me. He began to pray, and tears immediately spilled to my cheeks and the Holy Spirit came upon me. Then, he began to speak, I do not remember everything he said, but what I do remember made me weep more. He said, "That there were so many possibilities for my life and I could not begin to understand the possibility. You feel as if you are not enough and do not have it but you have possibility. In one month's time, one month something will happen or be revealed." This was not the first time that God has had this evangelist speak to me, but it was a word that was right on time. Almost a year before this service, he preached for us and he spoke these words to me, "I can see the hunger for more in your eyes. God is going to give you your desire(s)." And a year later God was doing great things in my life and leading me down a path to a new adventure. Now, a time frame was given that something was about to happen; therefore, I continued to wait upon God to show up in a mighty way within a month.

I waited... And nothing happened within the month but a month and half later something happened that shook me far more than it should have. The first Wednesday night of May, we had missionaries with us, and I was so happy to hear what they would preach or speak about. This service was very different from any other service we have had with missionaries before because my pastor called Taylor and I to come forward to be prayed for by the missionaries. We came forward and before the missionaries began praying for us he said, "There is a difference between a calling and a burden. We are going to pray for clarity." Then, he spoke directly to Taylor and said that she knew she had already been called. He just looked at me before he began praying for us. What he saw in those few moments I do not know. I began questioning myself and what I knew to be true. My mind turned against me in an instant and began to question whether I was called by God to missions or not. Those were fleeting thoughts as the missionaries began praying for us. He prayed for Taylor specifically, and his wife began praying with me. She whispered in my ear, "God has given you an ability, he is going to magnify it. Do not be afraid, do not fear." I thanked God for His word and I received it. However, the prayer was supposed to be for clarity, and I was even more discouraged and confused because I thought maybe Next Steps was not God's will but my own will. I was visibly shaken, and I spoke to Taylor about it outside after service that night. She was able to give me the perspective that I needed. However, I was still stressing over the situation at work the next day and broke down in my best friend, Kayla's classroom. When Taylor and

Kayla spoke almost the exact same advice to me, I chose to have faith that this was the right next step, and that I would receive clarity while on the mission trip.

After the service with the missionaries and questioning my next step, God provided assurance that I was on the right path the very next week. That next Tuesday, I received a phone call from the General Youth Division. The board members were on the phone to tell me the exciting news that I was a recipient of one of the $1,500 Sheaves For Christ scholarships. In that moment, all the doubts vanished when I received this news. This news was exactly what I needed to know that I was completely in the will of God. God knew in the back of my mind that I was a little worried about the finances for this trip. He expelled all fears and doubts. He is a faithful God, and is always listening to the prayers of His children. Now all that was left to do was to pack, and get ready to set off on a new adventure.

However, the Wednesday before I left for my trip to Scotland, I came down with a sickness that almost hindered me from leaving. I went to church that Wednesday night, and began feeling unwell, but I stayed until the end of prayer service. They called me forward to be prayed for before I left for my trip. In that moment, I did not know if I would make it home before I became ill. I did make it home, but I was so very sick for the next two days. I ran a fever, could not keep anything down including nausea medicine, and stayed either in bed or on the couch as I was very weak. Maybe it was just a bad case of the stomach virus, but no one else in the church came down with the stomach virus before or after, so I believe it was another attack against my health. However, even sickness could not keep me down. I made it to the airport with my bags, and I boarded that plane in New Orleans with Kimberly to fly to Washington, DC then on to Scotland. A new adventure was about to begin, and I was not about to miss what God was going to do in my life and the life of twenty-two others.

> *"The steps of a good man are ordered by the Lord:*
> *and he delighted in his way."*
>
> ~Psalms 37:23~

Laina M. Brown

Chapter Nine: Arrival in Scotland

There were so many emotions the day of departure, but thankfully I focused on the emotion of excitement instead of trepidation and anxiousness. As I said goodbye to my best friends in the New Orleans airport, I knew that things were going to change drastically in my life. I would never be the same person I was at that moment. I was prepared for what God was going to do in my life, or I thought I was prepared for my world to be turned upside down. The adventure was about to begin ready or not.

Our flight itinerary included a quick stop in Dublin to go through customs before flying on to Glasgow, Scotland. In our orientation, we were advised to go through customs alone if we had traveled in a group or with another person. When we got off the plane in Dublin, we went to the restroom as soon as we got off the plane instead of going through customs with a big crowd which was a mistake. By the time we came out of the restroom, we were the only two in line for customs, which did not bode well, because they had time to question us heavily about our plans in Scotland. They knew we were together when we tried to stay separate, so the customs agents became suspicious. People began to come up, so they told us to go sit down until they figured out what to do. In that moment, I was completely distraught on the inside, and I was trying to come up with a plan but to God be all the glory, they waved us back to the counter. They stamped our passports and allowed us to go through to get our bags and it was on to Scotland from there. However, I remained quiet from that point on because I was shaken, and it took me some time to realize that we made it through. I am the type of person that will go through all the scenarios of what could have happened in my mind even if they did not happen. We were really blessed and highly favored that day by God making a way, but there were others who were supposed to be with us on the trip, and the door was closed before arriving at the destination. However, God works everything for our good.

With just an hour plane ride from Dublin to Glasgow, we arrived in Scotland with all bags in tow. When we came through the sliding doors at the airport, we were met by some of the HBC students and the supervising representative. Other Next Steppers had arrived around the same time that Kimberly and I had arrived which was about 8-9am on Saturday, June 3rd. When everyone had arrived for the morning arrival, our representative took my suitcase and led us to the van they rented to transport us to our hostel. A short drive later we arrived at the hostel, but since we were so early our rooms were not prepared yet. Our supervising representative's wife and more HBC students met us at the hostel with reusable shopping bags full of authentic Scottish snacks and drinks. The hospitality we received was amazing. Since our rooms in the hostel were not ready yet, the hostel management allowed us to wait in the dining room until they were ready. Most of us were tired and fighting jet lag, but we were able to use the time to become acquainted some of the HBC students and the other few Next Steppers with us. Our rooms were not ready at lunch time, so we walked down to Subway which was on the same street as our hostel to get some lunch. By the time we finished eating, our room was ready, so a couple of the boys from HBC carried our luggage up the stairs to our third-floor room. They were so kind and chivalrous. Once we got to our rooms, we were able to shower and take a short nap while waiting for our other roommates to arrive before our first dinner with everyone else that evening.

When it was time, we got up from our naps and began to dress to meet everyone in the hostel lobby to walk to the Italian restaurant down the street for dinner. We enjoyed a great meal with everyone and were able to make new friends. I still remember sitting across from one of the other girls at the restaurant, and when she first heard my accent, she thought I was from Scotland I believe. It was truly a funny moment when I told her I was from Louisiana especially since she was from Texas. It was little moments like that that truly made the trip an amazing experience and connected everyone together like family. I was excited that I was going to have two of the young ladies I met on my first AYC trip as my roommates for the next month and one of whom was a great friend from that trip. Many more adventures were going to be made with each other and with our other roommates. Over the next month, we truly became like sisters in a huge family.

It may seem as if I am headed down a winding path, but just follow me for the point of this story is very much significant to why I titled this book "Walking by Faith, Not by Sight: The Mission of the Journey". In December of 2016, I was given a very special Christmas gift, from Taylor, with instructions not to open it until I made it on the ground in Scotland, not the airplane but in Scotland. And at the time the present was given to me, I had not heard whether I had been accepted to participate in Next Steps 2017. I was waiting for the news somewhat impatiently at that time because I was anxious to find out and waiting is one of my major weaknesses. Anyway, the Christmas present was a book titled "Jesus Calling". Taylor had tied a pretty yellow ribbon around the outside of the book and told me I was not to open it until I got overseas. In that moment, I began tearing up because her faith in God's plan for my life was so much higher than mine, and she will never realize how much I needed her faith to boost my own faith at that time. I did as she had asked and kept the book unopened until the night before we began classes in Scotland. As I untied that ribbon and opened the book a piece of paper fell out into my lap with Taylor's handwriting on it. That piece of paper was a lifeline and the encouragement that I needed. And to this day when I need encouragement or a reminder, I will remove that folded up piece of paper from between the pages of my Bible and read it over again. The words from that note will forever be an anthem in my soul, and little did I know then that it would be God's word for me in the years ahead. This is what Taylor's note said:

Dear Laina,

Today you open a new page of your life. You embark on a journey that will forever change your life! I always knew God had special things in store for you!

He has prepared you mentally, physically, and spiritually for this time in your life. Expect the greatest Laina. Expect for God to reveal himself to you in a way he hasn't before. Don't limit God or his abilities to do the supernatural in your life.

In every Christian's life sometimes things die within us that God has to awaken. God wants to awaken some old promises he has made you. He wants to awaken your faith. God is speaking to you Laina. Just hear him in the quiet moments.

Lord, bless my friend Laina today. Remove all fear, worry, and anxiousness. Help her to remember every promise you've ever made to her. I pray you would let your grace, love, comfort, and peace rest upon her from your throne room. Give her knowledge and wisdom of your will for her life today. Help her to walk by faith and not by sight. Lead her every step of the way.

Love, Taylor

The second to last sentence resonates within my soul every time I read it and was a common theme from my time in Scotland and Ireland. One night, when I mentioned about writing the book I always wanted to write, Taylor said, "I think you know what your book should be titled." As I sat there and thought about it, I was unsure of what the title should be then Taylor says "Walk by Faith, Not by Sight" and my reply was "You are right". Although I have adapted the original title, Taylor helped me in the beginning stages by encouraging my dream and helping me realize my potential with the help of God.

So, after reading the letter that night in my hostel bed, I was ready to step out on faith and find out what God had in store for my life. The God moments were in abundance the next few weeks. We watched as our lives were changed and how God truly was sending revival to Scotland.

"For as the body without the spirit is dead, so faith without works is dead also."

~James 2:26~

Walking by Faith, Not by Sight

Chapter Ten: Impactful Training

With the arrival in Scotland behind us, it was time for the training to begin. We had some of the best instructors to train us and inform us on culture, the EME region, and missionary life, but the best teacher we had was the Holy Spirit working through each instructor and student in the tabernacle. There were many times when God's spirit moved in our midst and spoke into our lives using willing vessels. In the beginning of the training, one of our instructors asked each one of us what was our desire to receive from the training and apprenticeship, and most of us hinted that we were seeking God's direction for our lives. So, the instructor had everyone to get a sheet of paper out and write down our goals for what we wanted to happen in our lives over and beyond the eight weeks. These were the goals I wrote and placed in my Bible:

1. *Grow stronger in my relationship with God.*
2. *Confirmation of the calling upon my life.*
3. *Confirmation of where I belong in the Kingdom of God.*
4. *Help with the works in the United Kingdom- To be available*
5. *Move out of my comfort zone by being bold in speaking and working for God.*
6. *Be a servant for God's Kingdom.*

These were the goals I was looking to accomplish. After we made our lists and verbalized that most of us were seeking direction, God answered ten-fold through tongues of interpretation, dreams, still small voices (God's voice), and sessions of revealing purpose. God had opened the door for this program for me, and He made sure that I did not doubt my purpose for being there.

Our first great move of God was our first Wednesday night service with the Scotland Church. A Scottish minister preached a message titled "From the Pit to the Rock." The entirety of his message was built upon the concept that God will never leave nor forsake you. During the altar service, there was a mighty wind of God's presence that swept through the tabernacle, and two different tongues of interpretation went forth. The first tongues of interpretation began with a question which said, "Have I not said that I will never leave nor forsake you? I have seen you in the darkness and the lonely times. I have not left you and I will never leave you." There was a second message which said, "I have plans for each of your lives and I will give you direction." God showed up in a mighty way by confirming to the ones seeking direction that He will provide it and that He will always be with us. This was only the first of many confirmations through His word. That very same night, I woke up from a dream and was paralyzed and could barely breathe. The dream was a very weird dream which had a representative's wife in it that I had met a few months prior and who had prayed over me. As I was staring at the representative's wife, something happened, and I began hearing a voice saying 'I will never leave nor forsake you... Do Not Fear.' As I heard it, I came closer to the woman and saw her face clearer. Then, I peered into the face of an animal that looked to be in the form of a dog but the face was evil. Then, I woke up to the fact that I could not move or breathe. I had no idea what was happening, but I spoke the name of Jesus in my mind and slowly I was able to breathe again to whisper the name of Jesus. After the name of Jesus was spoken, peace flooded into my spirit and I fell back asleep with only the memory of the ordeal the next morning. To this day, I do not know the reason I had that dream, but it certainly showed me that God is always with me especially when I call on the powerful name of Jesus.

Two days after the Wednesday night service and the dream, there was a phenomenal morning session titled "Marred Masterpiece" taught by a young woman. I am not ashamed to say that this session was one of my favorites because it spoke to my spirit from the first word that was uttered, and it was anointed for that time and hour. At the end of the session when she began praying, God's sweet presence blew through that church, and all I could do was lay my head down on the table and begin crying out in a heavenly language and openly weeping. My heart had been laid bare because God spoke to those dark places that I try to hide from everyone else. However, God was not finished speaking to us because we had tongues of interpretation come forth twice. A hush came over everyone and the tongues went forth then the interpretation which was: 'Thus saith the Lord, "I have called you, heed my call, heed my call."' Then another tongues and interpretation went forth where the Lord said, "Give yourself over to me." It was a powerful and eye-opening session which spoke into my spirit and confirmed some things but in true '*Laina fashion*' there was a tiny speck of doubt wondering 'Did He mean me when He said I have called you?' However, before training was over God made sure I had no doubts that He had called me.

Also, during this time, our assignments for the three weeks of apprenticeship were being decided. They had us choose where we would want to be placed, since we were going to be divided into groups to assist different representatives in Great Britain and Ireland. I did not really have a certain preference of where I wanted to be placed. I knew I would have liked to go back to Ireland, but I was comfortable with staying in Scotland to continue working with the church and representatives there. Initially, I was set to stay in Scotland, yet things changed when one of the instructors asked to talk to me on our way to training one morning. She asked me if I would be willing to complete my apprenticeship in Ireland to help the representative with a VBS since I had experience working with children and was a teacher at that time. So, I prayed about it. To be honest, I was not sure at first because I was afraid. However, after talking to a friend and receiving her advice, I had a sweet peace about going to Ireland. If I would not have listened to counsel and godly advice, I definitely would not be where I am today. Taking those small steps of faith was so important in this decision.

During our sessions the next week, we had many GOD moments. God truly was in the midst of His people during two of our sessions that day. The first impactful session was called 'Hearing God's Voice' taught by an inspiring instructor. She discussed how we can hear God's voice and we heard from God by the concept of praying a prayer, closing our eyes, and writing or drawing the first images and/or colors we see in our mind. Once all of our images or colors were combined, the big picture of what God was telling us was revealed by another instructor because she recognized the individual parts was identifying a specific person and the country they were working in at the time. Therefore, the next day we had prayer for that individual to give them strength to continue to make an impact where God had placed them. During the session titled "MK Ministries", she spoke about the big picture. Then we had another tongues of interpretation and God said, "I have called you. What more do you need? What more do you need? Do not be afraid my children. I am by your side." After the interpretation, the instructor said, "He chose you. You are here for a reason." God continued to confirm that He had called.

The other session we had that was incredible was called "Beyond Myself" where the needs of the nations and regions where addressed. There were stations arranged for each region of the world around the sanctuary. We were challenged to go to each region to pray and intercede for the needs that were listed. The presence of God was so tangible in the sanctuary as soon as we began praying. Just thinking back on that time in God's presence interceding for the nations, I am in tears. I wept, we wept, some were laid out on the floor face first. We all lost track of time and were not able to have our last session of the day because God truly came and met us in that room, truly an upper room experience like the day of Pentecost. God came and spoke again through tongues of interpretation, and this time He said, "I have called you for such a time as this. I am speaking to you and calling out to you." God's word and presence is always the reviving we need in our lives. It is like that old song says, *'Surely the presence of the Lord is in this place. I can feel His mighty power and His grace. I can hear the brush of angels' wings. I see glory on each face; Surely the presence of the Lord is in this place.'* It was an undeniable God experience that will never be forgotten.

In the midst of training and classes, we were attending church services, and God was speaking to us and the church members during this time. One particular altar call, we were all praying, and I was lost in the Spirit at the altar. Then, I heard a powerful still small voice that rang out "Don't Limit Me." Oh

Walking by Faith, Not by Sight

how I can still hear that phrase and voice in my mind as my Heavenly Father chastises me. The reminder of this phrase has continued to come forth from God in my life when I try to put limitations on what God can do in my life. For God is not limited, God is powerful and almighty. Our feeble minds declare our limitations and our weaknesses but that is not what God sees when He looks at us. He sees the purpose that He created us for and is waiting for us to heed His voice.

The third and final week of training brought new dimensions and we were introduced to two new instructors. One of the new instructors taught our first session on Monday morning titled "The Apostolic AIMer". In the beginning of the session, he revealed that God had spoke to him on May 21st about one of the Next Steppers and from that time he prayed for that person every morning as well as all the Next Steppers. Then he continued talking about the aspects of an Apostolic AIMer. At the end of the session, he had us pray with the person beside us, and I just had tears running down my face. He came to me and prayed for me. He gave me my confirmation from God that I needed because it was directed solely to me, and I could not doubt in those moments that God meant me, was speaking directly to me. The words he spoke from God were "I have called you and spoken to you. Small steps. Keep taking those small steps. He will open a door." God had called me, He was talking to me. Even though God had spoken repeatedly, I asked for more confirmation because I did not believe I was worthy of the calling that He was calling me to. And at the time I did not realize it, but I was still harboring self-esteem issues which hindered the work God wanted to do in my life. However, God did not give up on me because He has a purpose for my life, and He knows I have a determination to accomplish it by walking by faith. The other sessions of the week were very informative and encouraging. At the end of the week, we had completed all training and received our certificates on the Friday evening.

However, we had one more session before receiving our certificates that none of us were completely prepared for titled "Saying Goodbye Never Gets Easy". We had an experienced instructor in this topic teach this session to us and one of the most impactful things she said was "Don't cheat yourself by getting hung up on the goodbyes and hellos." Sometimes we have to say goodbye to things in our life so we can say hello to new things. By remembering this message, it has helped me to not worry over the goodbyes I will have to say throughout my mission journey because the hellos will always outweigh the goodbyes in my life. And most of my goodbyes will be 'see you soon' because I will always return home. Childhood home is home, and will not be replaced in my heart; however, other places, countries, and people will be part of my heart. I will find my other home, my mission's home. At the end of the session, our instructor began singing the song 'God Be With You Til We Meet Again' and we all gathered in a circle and sang it with her. I shed some tears because we formed a family and some of our family would be leaving soon to go back to the states and the Next Steppers would be moving on to each of our assignments in other nations. It truly was a bittersweet day and days ahead.

With training completed, we were about to go into our first week of apprenticeship with the supervising representatives at the Bible College to prepare for graduation but before we started a week of work, we had an amazing Sunday service. A minister preached a message titled "Bold Faith" and it spoke volumes. At altar service, an instructor came and prayed with me where I was standing in the pew. She said, "God give her a bold Faith. Replace the fear and doubt with boldness and anointing. You have a calling. God give her a boldness to do what you have called her to do." She poured into my life and spoke straight to my soul in those moments. She prayed, "Help her to step out in boldness and do the calling you have called her to do. Claim that faith, boldness, and anointing. We claim it right now Lord." I claimed all the things she prayed over me and prayed against fear and doubt in Jesus Name. I was so blessed to have amazing, Kingdom-minded Christians to pray with me and encourage me during this journey. I will forever be grateful for everyone that allowed God to use them to bless my life.

My last week in Scotland was spent being able to serve the church and the Bible College by cleaning, decorating, and cooking for the college graduation and reception. Many hours of work were put in to help prepare for the graduation, and it was worth it being able to watch all the students receive their diplomas that they had worked so hard to earn. However, our time in Glasgow was drawing to an end and we were about to go our separate ways. On Saturday night, we said goodbye to one of our instructor couples and daughter because they were leaving the next day. Our last night together as a Next Steps family was Sunday night. My roommates and I had been feeling the affects of spiritual warfare which came before we went to our assignments. In our room at the hostel, we decided to pray against that spirit and rebuke it in the name of Jesus. God's presence flooded that room, gave us peace, and renewed our unity. Then, one of my roommates spoke up that she felt that we should gather all the Next Steppers that night and pray a hedge of protection and unity within each group before we split up for our assignments, so we did. We gathered at the church in the common area of the boys' dorm and had a prayer meeting. God's presence came into the room and we had tongues of interpretation which said, "In these coming weeks, walk by faith and not by sight. You may not understand but walk by faith whatever may come. I have called you for such a time as this. Walk by Faith." A timely word that was needed during those next few weeks and even months in the future of adjusting back to life at home and missing the field. I have reminded myself of this word many times and it continues to be my prayer. This is another reason why this book is titled *Walking by Faith, Not by*

Sight: The Mission of the Journey. God continues to remind me to walk by faith and that life and missions is all about the journey, not the destination. Our ultimate destination is Heaven but Life... Life is a journey of walking by faith with God.

"For as the rain cometh down, and the snow from heaven, and returned not thither, but watereth the earth, and maketh it bring forth and bud, that it may give seed to the sower, and bread to the eater: So shall my word be that goeth forth out of my mouth: it shall not return unto me void, but it shall accomplish that which I please, and it shall prosper in the thing where to I sent it. For ye shall go out with joy, and be led forth with peace: the mountains and the hills shall break forth before you into singing, and all the trees of the field shall clap their hands. Instead of the thorn shall come up the fir tree, and instead of the brier shall come up the myrtle tree: and it shall be to the Lord for a name, for an everlasting sign that shall not be cut off." ~Isaiah 55: 10-13~

Laina M. Brown

Chapter Eleven: Operation Ireland

In the days leading up to leaving Scotland for Ireland, I had mixed emotions not because I did not have peace that I made the right decision to follow God's direction to Ireland; but I had grown accustomed to seeing my friends and being with the Next Steppers. Therefore, I confided in my best friend, Kayla, and asked her to pray that the emotions I was experiencing would leave so I could focus when I reached Ireland's soil. God answered those prayers and Operation Ireland began with trouble in immigration.

Immigration questioning always seems to be an issue for me. Maybe I look guilty or like I have a hidden agenda. It was surely an eventful 12am experience for me while the other Next Steppers waited to see if I made it out. My face must have given away my fear and shock once I joined the group again in baggage claim because I had worried faces surrounding me. Even the representatives had worried looks on their faces when we met them because we were delayed by my questioning. It was an ordeal which demonstrates where God made a way again. Immigration is not my friend but by God's grace, He will take care of all my future endeavors of entering a country.

I still remember all the emotions I had that night, and I was so grateful to arrive to the representative's house to lay down to sleep for the night. The next morning was July 4th, U.S. Independence Day. We prepared for the day ahead. We traveled with our host and his family to another representative's home for a 4th of July celebration. We were able to spend more time with the other Next Steppers who were serving with another representative in the south of Dublin. We were introduced to and spent time with some of the young people in the church. It was a day filled with fellowship, joy, and laughter as we enjoyed being with old friends and making new friends.

We attended Bible study with our representatives and was able to meet some of the church people. I was so nervous because I can be very awkward when meeting new people. Then we had to speak and introduce ourselves to everyone. I felt the heat creep up in my face when all eyes were on me as I spoke through my nerves. This was not the first time I would be called on to speak in front of everyone during my time in Ireland. That night we also moved in with one of the church families for the duration of our stay. We were tremendously blessed by this family for our stay.

One of our tasks during our apprenticeship with our host was to help with the church's VBS (summer camp). We spent our time preparing and working on creating crafts leading up to the VBS. We also cooked for the group who traveled from Louisiana to conduct the VBS. The VBS was a huge success. The children and adults all enjoyed the two days packed with fun activities and Bible stories. We were privileged to work with the children by teaching during their services.

After we had the VBS, we had a few days to sightsee, so we rented a car. We picked the car up Sunday morning before our service. I was our driver, and it was my first time driving on the left side of the road. We made it to the hotel safely but then there was an accident. The left side of the car got too close to a pillar in the underground garage, and it scratched the BMW. That was one of the worst moments, and I began to silently freak out though everyone could see it on my face. I was horrified. I learned a very valuable and expensive lesson that morning. When your mind is screaming at you to not try to park by a pillar, then LISTEN to it. To this day, everyone jokes about me leaving a mark in Ireland, and it is still a very visible mark. They have yet to paint over it, so everyone remembers the day I scratched that pillar.

That same day, our host representative entrusted us to lead the team from Louisiana around in Dublin City Centre, though, we had only been in the city centre a couple times. We made it to our destination thankfully. My sense of direction and memory was put to the test that day, and thankfully it did not fail me.

On Monday, we headed out for our road trip adventure to see the Cliffs of Moher and the city of Galway. Our road trip was filled with surprises and God's beautiful creation. The best moment was to walk the Cliffs of Moher as the sun was setting. It was such a serene experience, and I will cherish those memories. I felt I had arrived at the true Ireland that magnificent evening. I had already fallen in love with Ireland once before, but it just sealed my burden and my love for the country. There were so many other experiences and memories made on that two-day road trip including seeing the stately Kylemore Abbey in Connemara.

When we arrived back in Dublin, the church was still away on their camping trip, so we had a couple of days to discover more of the Dublin City Centre. We went to Trinity College to see The Long Room and the Book of Kells. Then we saw Dublin Castle and the Saint Patrick's Cathedral (all of the tourists' destinations). It was amazing being able to tour the great city of Dublin and receive a better sense of the culture.

On Sunday, we had service with our representatives' church, but we also went to South Dublin to be in service with the other Dublin representative's church. During altar call in the evening service, one of the ladies in the church came to pray with me and she spoke into my ear from the Lord about seeing myself the way that God sees me. She also said that I was beautiful (I cried, of course) which spoke volumes that within me I was still struggling with low self-esteem even though I thought that I had won the victory over those thoughts.

Admittedly, I was struggling with thoughts of inadequacy during that time because I let comparison creep into my mind. Those thoughts are one of my biggest struggles, but I choose repeatedly to speak life and God's promises over myself. May we all choose to do this when those thoughts come upon us. Let us speak God's word for it is our sword against the enemy.

The next week before we left Ireland, we were able to spend a day out with the young people of the church. We all met up at the shopping centre, purchased picnic food, and took a bus to Phoenix Park (which is the largest park in Europe). And we walked the entire park that day. I really wished I had worn different shoes because I had blisters on my feet by the end of the day. However, it was still one of the best days, and it was a joy getting to know the Ireland youth. After walking in the park, we took a bus from city centre back to the shopping centre where we met. We decided to play billiards and went bowling. Then, we ate dinner together at a restaurant. We were out until the sun went down and then it was time to say goodbye as we would not see them again before we left to fly home.

The last couple days left in Ireland were very difficult for me because I felt like my heart was breaking in pieces to have to leave again not knowing when I would ever come back. I went out alone for a walk the day before we left and sat under a tree in a park praying to God for His will. At the time, I also reached out to a friend back home and she replied with this statement:

"He puts the broken pieces together again, so you still have the scars to remember the hurt. You never forget a hurt like that; therefore, you never forget the cause." And with that statement of the day came my verse of the day from my Bible app which simply says, *"Let not your heart be troubled: ye believe in God believe also in me"* (John 14:1). God had spoken to my heart that day to not be troubled for everything was working out how it should.

Our God will always speak timely words into our spirits either through a friend or His word. Never forget that God knows exactly where we are. He is always trying to guide us and speak to us if we will only attend our ears to His voice and be sensitive to what thus saith the spirit.

"He that hath ears to hear, let him hear."
~Matthew 11:15~

Chapter Twelve: Not Goodbye, But See You Later

It came time to leave Dublin and travel back to Glasgow. That morning I hugged the representative's daughters bye and told the oldest daughter I would see her 'soon'. Not really realizing how true that statement would be in two days. When we flew back to Glasgow, we were able to meet back up with some of the other Next Steppers who would be flying to return home the next day as well.

We spent our last day in Glasgow by visiting a place to have afternoon tea and touring more of the city. It was a great day and time spent with friends. However, I had an apprehension in the pit of my stomach and to be honest I had the feeling the night before I left Dublin. The next day I would find out that I should have listened to that apprehension and what my mind was telling me to not fly back to Glasgow.

The next morning, we woke up and headed to the airport. I boarded my flight from Glasgow back to Dublin to catch my international flight. The entire one-hour flight from Glasgow, I continued to look at the clock. Time was not on my side, as I knew in my gut that I would not make my international flight. I had to go through immigration when we landed in Dublin and collect my bags then check them in for my other flight.

Remember before how I have trouble with immigration, well this immigration officer just looked at me with pity, stamped my passport, and let me go through. That look was that she knew I wasn't going to make my flight, and that was exactly what happened. I could not check my bags as the time had passed so they directed me to stand in line to rebook my flight.

While I was standing in the long line, I messaged my friend and mom to let them know I missed my flight then messaged the representative's wife to let her know as well. I finally made it to the desk to rebook my flight and I could not get another flight until the next day. I also had to book a separate domestic flight from Orlando to New Orleans since the airline could not change my domestic flight as well. I learned a very valuable lesson again about listening to that urging of what I should and should not do. However, God works everything together for our good (Romans 8:28).

The representatives came to the airport and picked me up. Their daughter said well that was really soon and is still a joke to this day. Since it was lunchtime, we went to eat at Nando's at the Pavilions shopping centre. While we ate, I also looked for domestic flights and booked a flight so I could let my friends know when I would arrive so they could meet me at the airport in New Orleans. Since, I was back in Dublin for the night, I let one of the youth know what happened. So, he invited me to come play tennis with some of the families of the church.

I was able to go and surprise them all when I walked up since only one or two knew I was coming. It was a great afternoon playing tennis and making friendships stronger.

I firmly believe God knew I needed that extra time in Ireland and was a way to provide a foreshadowing of what He had purposed for my life. Especially when the representatives came to pick me back up and the words spoken during that ride back to their home was a conversation God would later bring up to my mind during a confusing time in my life. There is purpose in every step taken, even when we may view it as a misstep at first.

"To every thing there is a season, and a time to every purpose under the heaven:"

~Ecclesiastes 3:1~

Laina M. Brown

Chapter Thirteen: Home with a Condition

Well, I finally made it on a plane heading to the land of my birth. There were some delays for my other flight once I made it to the states, but I finally landed in New Orleans around 11pm. As I was waiting for my luggage, my friends snuck up on me and squeezed me to death. It had been a long two months, yet it had also went by so quickly. I had missed them and was ready to see them since that was the longest I had ever been away from home. Knowing how timid I was years before, it can still be a shock knowing that God gave me the boldness to move out of my comfort zone. The call was more urgent than keeping myself feeling comfortable, and nothing miraculous happens in a stagnant comfort zone.

We made it back home in Jonesville early in the morning on a Sunday. Though I was jet lagged, I was determined to attend Sunday School that morning at my church. And God confirmed that I needed to be in attendance when the message my pastor preached went forward that morning. The sermon was based upon those words 'Faith and walking by faith.' It was exactly what my heart needed to hear as I just wept in the altar, I knew that my life would never look the same ever again.

I was home. It was true. Everything was the same. But I was different, and my heart hurt. Life continued though and moved on. I was due to begin another school year about two weeks after I returned. Dealing with the reverse culture shock was a real challenge because all I wanted to do was hop on the next plane back but I couldn't. Not yet anyway.

The school year began, and it was the most challenging of months. A job that I used to love presented so many challenges and discontentment that some days it was hard to keep it together. And one particular day, I broke down— sobbing— sitting in my classroom because I could not take the pressure to be strong any longer. Kayla and my mom just watched me that day and knew I had reached my limit. That moment opened my eyes that I no longer had a passion for my job. Looking back, it was a necessary break that had to occur for God to fulfill His purpose in my life. You see, I had projected that my future would be spent teaching at my old high school. At one time, I had everything I wanted. The doors had opened for me to get the position I wanted, but that was not what God wanted for my future. The pain and the break were God's way of pulling me out of that complacent place I was in and was not willing to loose my hold on before. Sometimes the breaking and the pain hurts so badly, but we must remember it is in the breaking where we are molded back together by the potter's hands into who He has created us to be.

Walking by Faith, Not by Sight

"But the pot he was shaping from the clay was marred in his hands; so the potter formed it into another pot, shaping it as seemed best to him. Then the word of the Lord came to me. He said, "Can I not do with you, Israel, as this potter does?" declares the Lord. "Like clay in the hand of the potter, so are you in my hand, Israel."

~Jeremiah 18:4-6 (NIV)~

Laina M. Brown

Chapter Fourteen: AIM or Not? And Where?

During the autumn and amidst dealing with work stress and challenges, I was battling spiritually between burden and desire verses clarity in direction and where to go. I was at another pivotal impasse in my life. The turmoil in my life was not just happening in the natural realm but in the spiritual realm as well. Until one day at work, one of my colleagues came and delivered some not so thrilling news which would be more difficult on all of us. I was already hanging on by a thread and the thread broke in that moment.

Since the students were testing that particular day, I had many hours to think and pray. Pray to God about what was happening in my life and why I felt like my world was breaking before my eyes. I had already been praying about an AIM term and missions. Everything happening kept seeming to draw me to AIM and away from everything I thought I wanted. So, in that classroom full of students testing on computers, a conversation I had with a representative came flooding back to my mind. In that moment, I felt strongly that applying for AIM was what God intended for me to do. However, I wanted complete confirmation so as soon as school had ended for the day, I drove to my church to pray. I needed alone time with God to seek and search for His will.

When I reached the church, one of the ministers was in his new office which is close to the church's prayer room. I went to the prayer room, knelt down, and began to pray earnestly. During that time as I was seeking answers and for God's confirmation to apply for AIM in Ireland, someone touched me on my shoulder. I hurriedly turned around to glance, but no one was there so I turned and faced the back of the pew I was kneeled before. I still felt the barest sensation of where someone had touched my shoulder and I felt such peace in my soul. What I thought might have been the minister who was studying in his office, was in fact an angel and my confirmation that God was leading me. My next steps would be to obtain wisdom and approval from spiritual leaders and apply for the AIM term that God was leading me to.

The months leading up to this moment were necessary though very painful. As God stripped away the desire and orchestrated the events that would lead me to no longer wish to teach in a public school but replaced it with a desire for missions and a different type of education. My passion changed from influencing the minds of teenagers to striving to achieve a different kind of influence in the lives of people around the world.

It was God's time for me to take another leap of faith and trust him again as I was getting ready and willing to walk away from a job and family for the truth to be known... the complete unknown. It was the unknown, but it quickly became the known as God's leading carried me in the right direction, a direction of obedience.

"Teaching them to observe all things whatsoever I have commanded you: and, lo, I am with you always, even unto the end of the world. Amen."
~Matthew 28:20~

With following after the Lord's commandment and leading, there were some hindrances. Anytime pursuing after the call of God, there will be obstacles; wisdom and knowledge will be needed to overcome. However, God made a way as He always does when it is His will for His children. Only God can open and shut the doors in our lives, and this is a door that He had surely opened, and no man could shut.

During this prolonged period, I had a couple of dreams yet one dream in particular was very vivid. This dream was very bright, and it was of me back in Ireland at the representatives' house. At the time, I did not realize how important the dreams I was having would be until a couple months later. As I did not have the discernment that the dreams might have been God dreams when they happened, but I did not soon forget those dreams as I had other dreams before.

"For in the multitude of dreams and many words there are also divers vanities: but fear thou God."
~Ecclesiastes 5:7~

"The prophet that hath a dream, let him tell a dream; and he that hath my word, let him speak my word faithfully. What is the chaff to the wheat? Saith the Lord." ~Jeremiah 23:28~

Chapter Fifteen: God, AIM Training?

The AIM application had been sent and it was time to wait for approval. During this time, Global Missions had announced AIM Training the beginning of January 2018. I did not know whether I should try to attend or not. I had a desire to attend but it was right after New Year's and the weekend before I went back to work from Christmas break. The finances were also part of my decision as my dad told me that before I took another long trip anywhere in my car, I would have to buy new tires. And tires are expensive, so this fact made me lean in the direction of not attending. I was also thinking about a future budget I would need to raise if I was accepted to AIM in Ireland. However, I decided to fast, pray, and fleece the Lord about His will in attending AIM training.

It was slowly coming upon the last day to register for AIM training the beginning of December. So, I told the Lord that if I received correspondence about AIM training before the registration date ended that I would register and go no matter the extra expenses needed to make it happen. Well, I received an email about AIM training while I was at work, a few hours after I told that to the Lord. So, I said okay "Lord, I will register." Then, I contacted Taylor to see if she would be willing to go with me as I did not want to travel alone to St. Louis. Then, I called my mom and let her know that I would be registering and going, and that I would just cover the expenses and trust God.

Taylor decided to go with me, so I registered both of us for AIM training the beginning of January. A few hours after that I received a message that our stay in the hotel in St. Louis would be covered and we would not have to pay for it. I sat in 'Awe' for several minutes at the generosity of this person but at the awesomeness of my God. For this person said that God spoke to them to cover our hotel costs. In those moments without a doubt God wanted us at this training, and great things would come out of it.

"Let us hold fast the profession of our faith
without wavering; (for he is faithful that
promised;)"

~Hebrews 10:23~

During this time before the holidays, another option was presented to me by my representatives in Ireland about my AIM term. My plan was to return in the summer of 2018 if I was approved and my budget was raised. However, they suggested I wait another year and come as they could use my help in 2019 when it was their deputation time. So, we all decided to begin praying and see where God led. A few months later in March God gave me the decision through words of confirmation about when to return to the field. It was not necessarily what I planned or wanted to be honest, but it was all about God's timing and His will.

"For it is God which worketh in you both to will and to do of his good pleasure."

~Philippians 2:13~

Laina M. Brown

Chapter Sixteen: AIM Training 2018

The time for AIM training had finally arrived. Time to make the long trek to St. Louis. Taylor and I had great expectations for the training as we knew in our spirits that God was going to move in a great way and there would be clarity and direction imparted during the weekend of training.

We left early Thursday morning so we could arrive in St. Louis with enough time to prepare for the evening kick-off service for AIM training. For me driving all day was exhausting physically but my spirit was ready to receive divine words from God. We arrived at Headquarters for the night service, and as soon as we walked in the door, we were greeted by smiling, friendly, and familiar faces. There were several mission-minded friends I have met over the years and many were Next Steps family from the summer before. It was so uplifting to see them all again and be able to worship together again during the training.

That night we had an amazing speaker and a great move of God. The next day we had an early start, and began our day of powerful training sessions as well as being able to visit with multiple regional directors to gain insight from their experiences and passion for their respective regions of service. Though we had multiple messages that spoke to the hearts of the participants, one of the most memorable moments of the entire training was when we formed a prayer line at the end of one of the sessions. For that is when God spoke to my hurting heart and assured me that He has always had a plan for my life.

After I had gone through the prayer line, reached the end of the line, I had two amazing young women come to me, hug me and speak words of encouragement directly from God into my spirit. The first word from God was regarding that dream I mentioned at the end of the last chapter. She said, "You have been given a dream and that dream is about to be manifested in your life. It is going to happen." In that moment, I just cried even more while lost in the Holy Spirit because I knew she did not know that I had that dream a couple months before. Then, a few minutes later, another young woman came to me and said, "You have a great anointing." And that broke me over again because God knows just the words to speak at just the right time. For the doubt I had about even being able to be used, and equipped to be used by God dissipated in those moments with those few words spoken.

"But the anointing which ye have received of him abideth in you, and ye need not that any man teach you: but as the same anointing teacheth you of all things, and is truth, and is no lie, and even as it hath taught you, ye shall abide in him."

~1 John 2:27~

The anointing which God hath given is the truth and it shall teach you, equip you to walk in the Spirit. We must never doubt what God has given each of us. Never doubt the anointing that He has given to each one of us. We all must go through a crushing process to produce the oil of anointing, which is why our individual anointing in areas will be different from others.

Again, the Lord had spoken words into my life to continue pressing my mission journey forward and His will for my life. Though some battles were fought that weekend and molding to my heart was taking place, God spoke to confirm that I was in the potter's hands and moving in the direction of His will and plan. God made a way for us to attend the training because He had specific words and challenges to place before us during the season to come.

"I know thy works: behold, I have set before thee
an open door, and no man can shut it: for thou
hast a little strength, and hast kept my word, and
hast not denied my name."

~Revelation 3:8~

Laina M. Brown

Chapter Seventeen: BOTT 2018

After the AIM training, we returned home, and I went back to work the next day. On the way home from St. Louis, I decided that I needed to begin a week-long fast on Monday to gain some clarity, insight and to die to self. It certainly was not an easy fast, but fasting is not supposed to be comfortable or easy. When the fast was over, God did a work in me as well as prepared my spirit to receive at the BOTT 2018 conference.

I had attended a couple of night services at BOTT in past years, but this was the first year where I would be attending all services, day sessions and night services. I was able to register and took off work for a few days to attend. My dad, who is the best dad, had brought their camper to the Tioga campgrounds the Saturday before the conference so I could stay close to the city instead of commuting an hour one way for the services. It was ready, set, go for the conference.

The week of the conference came and the excitement and expectancy were so tangible. I knew God was going to do many great works in this impactful conference for ministers and leaders, but I could not have fathomed the things God spoke directly to me during that week. God was definitely speaking to my heart and knew that I needed those words to ignite my boldness to move forward.

The Tuesday morning of the beginning of the conference, I had registered for the leadership forum to receive more imperative leadership training. It was great training and very informative. However, insecurity began to resurrect within me as I sat alone for the training. It began to sink in that as I was moving forward, I could not bring people, my people with me for this journey. And that was a scary aspect. Though I had dealt with these feelings before going on multiple mission trips where I could not bring friends and family with me, it began to sink in on a larger scale because of where God was leading me. Being at BOTT, among the missionaries and not sitting with my Pastor (part of my security), it was foreshadowing a future reality of leaving all familiar behind for the unknown. That insecurity, fear and doubt is what God would deal with me about during this momentous week.

The first night of BOTT was a powerful service and God's presence was imminent and palpable in that auditorium. I had found a seat in the missionary section and God has a sense of humor or just orchestrates things perfectly for that night I sat by another AIMer (Associate in Missions) who had served in— you will not guess—Ireland. I thought to myself in that moment, 'This is not a coincidence and God you are Good.' We talked before the service began and became connected. She became another person that I could ask about some AIM questions in the future. Everything else that took place that week just provided more evidence that God was in control and leading my steps, just as He told me to keep taking those small steps.

The next morning, we had great morning services. There was a move of the Holy Spirit, and we were praying one with another. In the midst, I had a man of God lay his hand on my head and spoke encouragement to my life as I sobbed while lost in the Holy Spirit. Then all of a sudden, another person took hold of my hand and spoke these words with authority in the Spirit, "Quit doubting the dreams." I broke down sobbing even more. I never saw who spoke those imperative words in the Holy Spirit, but I sincerely thank them for following God's leading. Remembering those few moments and words still brings tears to my eyes. Once again, God revealed Himself in awe inspiring ways.

"But the Comforter, which is the Holy Ghost, whom the Father will send in my name, he shall teach you all things, and bring all things to your remembrance, whatsoever I have said unto you."
~John 14:26~

The Lord surely reminded me that He was speaking to me and leading me. God will send confirmations in many forms, and the confirmations that He sends will show His Glory and be undeniable in ways that can only come from our Heavenly Father. If God has spoken to you, don't doubt nor fear just trust and wait upon Him.

One of the last messages preached at the conference was centered upon Ezekiel and the valley of dry bones. This story is a very familiar one for most Christians as we have heard it used in many sermons. However, one phrase that the preacher spoke rooted itself into my heart. He said, "The change that God wants to do in the dry place is about to take place." How true that statement was and a word for the church. Our God specializes in deliverance from our dry places, from our wildernesses but that place, that wilderness must be walked through for the growth, the change to happen in you. The change and growth will always, always be worth any and all discomfort during the dry place because God will speak life and give breath into it again.

"Thus saith the Lord GOD unto these bones;
Behold, I will cause breath to enter into you, and
ye shall live:"

~Ezekiel 37:6~

Chapter Eighteen: Not My Timing, God's Timing

At the beginning of February 2018, I received official word that my AIM extension was approved to return to Ireland. I was so ecstatic, elated, and all other synonyms that can express joy unspeakable. God had opened this door, and I was ready to walk through it no matter the cost or sacrifice. However, at that time I did not know the journey to standing on Ireland soil again would not be easy. Was I expecting easy? Well to be honest, I did not know what I expected but I knew it was going to be much work involved, especially to raise and save my substantial budget. The main thing I expected, well wanted, was to be in Ireland June 2018 but God... say it again... but God had other plans. Remember, our thoughts and plans are not God's thoughts and plans.

During this time of receiving the news, there was a missions conference in another city that I had attended with some friends. We drove the two hours to one of the night services. At the altar call of this service, I had someone come and pray for me. They spoke that 'God is about to give you hope and this is your year.' While they were praying for me, God brought back to my mind a vision that I had the Sunday before at church and showed me the meaning of it. The vision was of me hanging between two cliffs and in that moment, it was like

God whispered "You are trying to cling to home and missions when I just need you to surrender all to the call placed on your life." I felt chastised like a little child because I was trying to do that very thing not realizing how it was hindering the call and anointing God wanted to work in my life. Living the surrendered life is the only way; for the word of God says that we cannot serve two masters for we will love the one and hate the other.

"No man can serve two masters: for either he will hate the one, and love the other; or else he will hold to the one, and despise the other. Ye cannot serve God and mammon."

~Matthew 6:24~

As I was determined to live a surrendered life and not cling to things or people who could not go with me where God was leading, the next couple months contained some searching and seeking God's will on timing. I wanted to return to Ireland as soon as possible, but God spoke to me through my Pastor's words one Sunday night in March to confirm in my spirit that I needed to wait. I, like any other child, pouted about having to wait but accepted God's will and said let it be done. So, wait is what I did and so many things happened during that year of waiting.

After the decision to wait another year before leaving for Ireland, I went to a neighboring church's conference that they have every year. Since my pastor was preaching the Friday morning of the conference, I decided to take off work because I felt like I needed to attend, and I would rather attend service than go to work that Friday. There was a reason why I felt in my spirit that I should attend, God had a word for me that day. As the first speaker preached, I sat on the pew with tears in my eyes because the words spoke volumes to how I was feeling spiritually. Then my Pastor began preaching and he was on fire that morning. When it was time for altar call, I went to the front but stood behind others worshipping. Then a man came over to the woman's side and told me to come further upfront, he had the other women gather around me and he laid his hand on my head and began praying. As I began speaking in other tongues through the Holy Spirit, tears rolled down my face while they all prayed for me. It was a powerful uplifting that I needed but the word that I needed came at the end when a familiar friend came up to me as we were leaving. He said, "I may be way off but when they were praying for you all I could see was the word 'Purpose' in my mind. I wanted to tell you that your purpose was about to be fulfilled." And that word was why I felt like I needed to be at that service that morning regardless of other responsibilities that I needed to be doing during that time. God spoke another word, another piece in the steps that I was taking.

"For we are saved by hope: but hope that is seen is not hope: for what a man seeth, why doth he yet hope for? But if we hope for that we see not, then do we with patience wait for it."

~Romans 8:24-25~

The next few months brought laughter and sorrow at work and at home. One particular night in April, my friends and I decided to have a late-night prayer meeting at the church because we knew a transition was taking place in each of our lives and we all needed answers, words from God. During that prayer meeting with just the three of us, God met us and spoke through tongues of interpretation into all of our hearts. The words spoken from God said, "Stop trying to figure it out. Stop trying to understand. Stop trying to do it on your own. My ways are higher, I can see further than you can see. When the time comes, I have already made the provision, but you can't do it on your own." Those very poignant words were reminders to each of us in our own situations. In my situation of budget raising and missions, God reminded me once again that He is in control and sees more than I can see which is why I must continue to 'Walk by Faith, not by Sight'.

Just a few weeks later in May, I decided to apply for another teaching position in another district after much prayer. I took a step of faith, and prayed for God's will to be done in the situation. It was time to let go of the dream that I had of teaching at my old high school for the rest of my life. God was already calling me away from that, and I needed to step away into another atmosphere. So, at the end of the school term, I brought my application and resume to apply elsewhere for a year before leaving for the field. When God opens another door, it is time to step through it with many expectations.

> *"My soul, wait thou only upon God; for my expectation is from him."*
>
> *~Psalms 62:5~*

Laina M. Brown

Chapter Nineteen: 2018 Summer Transition

Though there was a transition taking place spiritually back in the spring, summer 2018 brought many different physical transitions, moves, along with spiritual transition. A portion of the summer was a dedicated waiting game, and albeit a dreading not knowing where I would be come the fall term. Longsuffering was not a fruit of the Spirit that I was exhibiting during that time though I tried.

Along with waiting game I was experiencing, I had allowed myself to become numb spiritually and emotionally. I was numb on the inside and did not know why. Maybe I had created a coping mechanism so I would not be disappointed or probably the main reason is that I no longer wanted to feel pain because it hurt too much. It was not long before I received an answer to why I felt numb and isolated.

In June, my friends and I, just the three of us again, were at Taylor's house talking. We decided to have another prayer meeting, and this time it was a midnight prayer meeting. All three of us began praying in different rooms of the house. As I sat in a curled ball on the couch, I could not find the words to pray, nor could I utter hardly a word though I was thinking in my mind. As I began fighting through the numbness in my spirit, Taylor spoke that she felt in her spirit that God was about to speak to us, so we went to the upstairs room (the upper room) where Kayla was. We all began to intercede, and the Holy Spirit swept into that room so strongly. There were tongues of interpretation and we all ended up laying/sitting on the floor weeping and speaking in a Heavenly language. I came to and began singing a song that was on my heart then they joined in singing. Then we all got quiet. Taylor began speaking in tongues. During the tongues, she spoke my name in the midst of the tongues and came over to me. She laid her hand on my forehead and said from God, "You've prayed Lord why this pain I have felt always. How many times do I have to tell you that I will do what I said I will do? Glory in the sufferings. Did you think that you would have anointing without the sufferings?" And more was spoken but it was such a powerful presence and anointing that I began weeping uncontrollably in the Holy Spirit. God truly visited with us that night and spoke directly to me. 'Glory in the sufferings.' I still remind myself of this phrase today as well as the scripture Paul wrote in Romans.

Walking by Faith, Not by Sight

"By whom also we have access by faith into this grace wherein we stand, and rejoice in hope of the glory of God. And not only so, but we glory in tribulations also: knowing that tribulation worketh patience; And patience, experience; and experience, hope: And hope make the not ashamed; because the love of God is shed abroad in our hearts by the Holy Ghost which is given unto us. For when we were yet without strength, in due time Christ died for the ungodly."

~Romans 5:2-6 (KJV)~

*"Not only so, but we also **glory in our sufferings**, because we know that suffering produces perseverance; perseverance, character; and character, hope."*

~Romans 5:3-4 (NIV)~

There was another prayer meeting that took place in July. My friend called me and asked if I could meet her and our other friend at the church to pray, so I readily said yes. I decided to go to the church early to pray alone before the meeting time. I needed some alone time with God, just me and Him, as I was struggling and needed to just be in communion with my Savior. When they arrived, we went to the church's prayer room to pray together over a specific situation. However, during that prayer meeting to pray for a friend's need God used her to speak into my life, which was just very surprising, because I did not expect it and no one knew what she spoke, only God did. For it had been weeks that I was having sleepless nights and when sleep did come it was filled with dreams of discouragement. Not knowing this fact, this friend looked me directly in the eyes and said, "The spirit of fear, anxiety, depression and unworthiness has attacked and if you don't let it go your mind is going to be the devil's playground. The sleeplessness and fear have plagued you. Let go of all the things people have said in your past to hurt you. You are worthy. It will hinder the call on your life if you don't let go of it." In that instant she finished those words, I acted by getting to my feet, dancing and commanding those spirits to flee in Jesus Name as well as claiming victory.

God is so good. He uses people and works through them to speak words of encouragement and speak into situations that only He knows about. Never underestimate the power of God to use people in your life. We all have to continuously be willing vessels for God to use at a moment's notice. And we never know how the urging of the Spirit to speak to someone will impact their day, their month or even their life. Those words spoken revealed what I was battling with spiritually so I could find the right words to pray over myself and my mind. Be that willing vessel and have faith and boldness to speak when the Spirit urges you to do so.

*"Now, Lord, consider their threats and enable your
servants to speak your word with great boldness."
~Acts 4:29 (NIV)~*

It was not long after this prayer meeting that I received a call for a job interview at a junior high school in another town.

God had opened up the door for another position, but I continued to pray for God's will because I could only commit to working a year. I went into the interview the next week being open about the fact that after a year I would be leaving to do missions work. I came out of the job interview with the job. God had opened that door not only for me but also my best friend received a job offer at the same school. We would be starting and teaching together at the same school. God was so good to us and allowed us to move schools and continue working together. The next few weeks consisted of making this transition and preparing for the new school year in a very different environment. New experiences were on the horizon.

Before we began the school year though, we planned a trip to attend two different conferences at the beginning of August. We attended Apostolic Conference in Madison, Mississippi then traveled to Little Rock, Arkansas to attend a camp meeting. The last night of Apostolic Conference I prayed a prayer for God to purge me of anything that was not His will for my life or that needed to be taken out of me. God began doing a work on me that week and I felt like my heart was being squeezed. Everything I saw or did reminded me of my burden, of my calling and my country I was longing to be in. I quickly realized that I did not belong where I was any longer, but God had a work to finish in me. We went to a home missions church and the presence of God was so strong in that small church. It was as if God whispered during the worship service when others prayed with me that this is more like home, missions. My heart continued to ache as I thought of home, my missions home. I was in a time of heart reconstruction that could not be explained and dealing with spiritual battles. During this time a specific scripture became my anthem to whisper when the battle was so overwhelming. *"Submit yourselves therefore to God. Resist the devil, and he will flee from you"* (James 4:7). I had to remember to continue to submit myself to God's will, and the lies and deceptions from the evil one would leave for the devil does not like when you are glorying God.

> *"But he give the more grace. Wherefore he saith, God resisteth the proud, but give the grace unto the humble. Submit yourselves therefore to God. Resist the devil, and he will flee from you. Draw nigh to God, and he will draw nigh to you. Cleanse your hands, ye sinners; and purify your hearts, ye double minded."*
>
> *~James 4:6-8 (KJV)~*

We arrived home from this trip and the battle within was still waging but God was fighting my battles and maturing me in the process. Then the new school year at a different school began, and it was a learning process as there were new policies and procedures to learn and teach. However, during this time a curveball at home took place, my youngest nephew and niece came to live with us, and it became our responsibility to raise them. It was a major adjustment for my parents and I, but we knew they needed to be with us. The last transition in this summer of major transition and growth. God knew exactly what He was doing, and it was all in preparation for the next season. In hindsight, God needed me to be home in Louisiana with my family. There was a season that needed to take place during that extra year of not being on the field.

> *"For then shalt thou lift up thy face without spot; yea, thou shalt be steadfast, and shalt not fear: Because thou shalt forget thy misery, and remember it as waters that pass away: And thine age shall be clearer than the noonday; thou shalt shine forth, thou shalt be as the morning. And thou shalt be secure, because there is hope; yea, thou shalt dig about thee, and thou shalt take thy rest in safety. Also thou shalt lie down, and none shall make thee afraid; yea, many shall make suit unto thee."*
>
> *~Job 11:15-19~*

Laina M. Brown

Chapter Twenty: Undeniable GOD Moments

During the fall of 2018, I traveled back to St. Louis twice for a missions conference and training. It was a busy time but a time of preparation. The first conference was Global Connextions 2018 in October. Then in November, I traveled back to attend TESOL training I had registered to take to receive certification to teach English as a second language.

Global Connextions was another phenomenal conference. It was a great time of fellowship, mission connection and anointed messages from God. I was able to see and spend time with many Global minded friends I have met along the way of this mission journey. After these few days of listening to Words from God, I came away knowing that I needed to be bold by talking to my Pastor again and share my burden with my home congregation. It was time to do the one thing I am not confident in doing and that is speaking in front of a congregation, but God gave me the words and strength to do so. My Pastor allowed me to speak the first Wednesday night of December and share my testimony and burden. My mother told me later that she did not recognize me as it was like I was a different person which let me know that God surely took over and anointed the words.

The new year, 2019, brought some challenges as I was switched to a different teaching position at my job which was an adjustment trying to prepare the students for state testing. In the midst of this challenge, I was trying to finish raising my budget, and praying about a visa as the door seemed closed in regard to staying a year on the field. These two factors seemed to be constant in my mind and in my prayers. The plane ticket was booked for June, so I just needed these two things to be in order.

One of the undeniable God moments during this time was when God spoke a direct word to me immediately after I was overthinking about my budget. One morning, I woke up trying to control and analyze what I needed to do to raise the rest of my budget. Grandmother was at our house that morning when I went to fix my morning coffee, so I talked to her before going to do my Bible reading. And she spoke a word from God to me. She said, "God is going to provide. You may not have everything you want but you will always have everything that you need." After she spoke those words, I went to pray and just cried because I knew in that moment that whenever doubt would try to creep in that I could hold on to the promise God had given me that day for my confirmation.

*"Therefore I say unto you, Take no thought for
your life, what ye shall eat, or what ye shall drink;
nor yet for your body, what ye shall put on. Is not
the life more than meat, and the body than
raiment? Behold the fowls of the air: for they sow
not, neither do they reap, nor gather into barns;
yet your Heavenly Father feedeth them. Are ye not
much better than they?*

~Matthew 6:25-26~

Honestly, I must say that during this time I had an inner dialogue of doubt and fear. I knew what God had spoken, that He had provided and opened this door. However, I had circumstances in life which made me wonder if I should leave my home and my parents to take care of my niece and nephew alone. I felt sincere responsibility to continue helping in the care of my brother's children yet the urging to return to the field was so strong. Though not many knew, I was conflicted and battling whether I should leave home but God.

Yes, I was internally struggling with family responsibility and God's calling, yet I was still planning to leave in June for the field. My best friend and I had planned a trip to New York City during spring break as it was our dream to see a broadway play on broadway, and we wanted to do it before I left and things changed. While we were in New York City, we wanted to see the 911 Memorial, so we took the subway to see it. When we came off of the subway onto the street, we were greeted by this man who was selling books about 911. He stopped us and was talking to us. To be honest, I was a little leery when he first began talking. Yet, he told us that he was a born again Christian, and that he could see we were Christians because we had the Holy Spirit shining on our faces. Then he asked us how long we had been in church and we replied with "all our lives". The next statement he made shocked me to the core. He said that he could tell we had been and that we would be a missionary and preacher's wife in our future. After he said that I had no words, I just looked at my friend with big eyes. He just had no idea how true he was; considering, I would be leaving for the mission field in just a little over a month. That moment, that word served as another confirmation from God that I was walking in the direction God wanted for my life. A truly undeniable God moment happened on a packed New York City street with a word from a stranger. The scripture about "Entertaining angels unawares" became alive for me that day.

"Be not forgetful to entertain strangers: for thereby some have entertained angels unawares."
~Hebrews 13:2~

The next month was spent finishing some preparations to leave for the field by resigning from my job and selling my car. It was also spent by spending as much time with my family as I could. My grandfather's health was declining from battling cancer. The diagnosis from the doctors was not promising as they did not give him much longer, so we were at my grandparents' house as much as possible at the end of May. We were all with my grandparents the Thursday before I was to leave. As I sat by my grandfather, he asked me when I was leaving and I said, "I leave on Tuesday morning, Pawpaw." He just nodded at me. And those were the last words I spoke to my grandfather as he went to be with his Savior in the wee hours of Friday morning. Before I had left my grandparents' house that Thursday evening, my uncle and aunt talked to me because they knew it was bothering me that I might not be home to be with the family when my grandfather passed. They wanted me to understand that it would be okay if I wasn't there for the funeral and that we could have the service broadcasted online so I would be there. However, God chose to call him home and I was able to have the closure and say goodbye in person before I said goodbye to everyone else.

God's timing is always perfect. I will be forever grateful for that time that I had with my family before I fully stepped into the next season of my life. And that Tuesday morning was the day I would take a step of faith into the biggest adventure I had ever been on. The goodbyes and see you laters were said. It was time for take off. So, I stepped into destiny with God when I put my feet onto that plane heading to a foreign land which would become HOME.

> *"And we know that all things work together for good to them that love God, to them who are the called according to his purpose." ~Romans 8:28~*

Laina M. Brown

Author's Note

Hello Readers! If you have made it to this page, then you have probably finished reading this portion of God's journey for me. May the scriptures used throughout this book from God's Word continue to resonate within your heart and soul for days to come for they are His promises to us all. Thank you from the bottom of my heart for choosing to read my experiences that God has blessed me with.

In the future, I pray to be able to share even more with you about the goodness of our Heavenly Father. If you have enjoyed reading about my story and would like to read more, I have a blog titled 'Adventures with Laina' which you can find on Wordpress. Again, thank you to my readers for without you and God this would not be possible. May God bless you all abundantly. Go forth and pursue the journey that God has for your life. Remember, God did not give a spirit of fear so pursue boldly what God is speaking to your heart and walk boldly in the anointing from the Holy Spirit.

Special Note: During the process of editing this book, Grandmother, a mighty prayer warrior, went to be with Jesus. She will be forever greatly missed, but she left a legacy in her children and grandchildren. I am grateful for her love, support, and prayers. We will love you forever, Grandmother. Until we meet again in our Heavenly Home.

Laina M. Brown

Acknowledgements

This book would not be what it is without some very important key people who have helped in making this dream possible as I could not have completed it on my own. They deserve so much more than just an acknowledgement and credit, but I pray that they will see my sincere appreciation of their talents through my words.

Sister Maria, thank you for your support and encouraging me to "Go for it!" I appreciate your guidance in my life.

Tonya (mom), thank you for being the first one to read the very rough draft of this book and editing my grammar as it can get very messy. Also, thank you for encouraging me through your words after reading the book.

Kayla, thank you so much for your time, effort, and dedication to be my editor. Your editing and suggestions have immensely improved the overall quality and message of this book. I appreciate your help, support, and talent.

Kromwell, I appreciate your willingness to create the cover art for this book. You are so talented in digital art so I knew you would be the person I could trust to create an amazing work of art. And that is what you did! Thank you so much from the bottom of my heart.

Laina M. Brown

About the Author

Laina M. Brown is originally from Jonesville, Louisiana. She lives in Dublin, Ireland at this time serving in missions and is a member of The Family Church of Ireland. Laina has obtained a BA in English from Louisiana State University of Alexandria and is currently pursuing a BA in Business at CCT college in Dublin. She loves spending her time being a servant in the Kingdom of God. She values time spent with God, family, and friends. Some of her favorite things are drinking coffee and reading. She has a blog called 'Adventures with Laina'. She desires to encourage and inspire whoever she can with the words and experiences God has granted her.

Laina M. Brown

Printed in Great Britain
by Amazon